3

NEW DIRECTIONS IN THEATRE

General Editor   JULIAN HILTON

D0527652

WITHDRAWN FROM
THE LIBRARY

UNIVERSITY OF
WINCHESTER

'004

KA 0230127 X

NEW DIRECTIONS IN THEATRE

Published titles

FEMINISM AND THEATRE
Sue-Ellen Case

IMPROVISATION IN DRAMA
Anthony Frost and Ralph Yarrow

PERFORMANCE
Julian Hilton

NEW DIRECTIONS IN THEATRE
Julian Hilton (*editor*)

POSTMODERNISM AND PERFORMANCE
Nick Kaye

THEATRE AS ACTION
Lars Kleberg

A SEMIOTICS OF THE DRAMATIC TEXT
Susan Melrose

TRANSPOSING DRAMA
Egil Törnqvist

Forthcoming titles

REPRESENTATION AND THE ACTOR
Gerry McCarthy

Postmodernism and Performance

NICK KAYE

© Nick Kaye 1994

All rights reserved. No reproduction, copy or transmission of
this publication may be made without written permission.

No paragraph of this publication may be reproduced, copied or
transmitted save with written permission or in accordance with
the provisions of the Copyright, Designs and Patents Act 1988,
or under the terms of any licence permitting limited copying
issued by the Copyright Licensing Agency, 90 Tottenham Court
Road, London W1P 9HE.

Any person who does any unauthorised act in relation to this
publication may be liable to criminal prosecution and civil
claims for damages.

First published 1994 by
THE MACMILLAN PRESS LTD
Houndmills, Basingstoke, Hampshire RG21 2XS
and London
Companies and representatives
throughout the world

ISBN 0–333–51917–5 hardcover
ISBN 0–333–51918–3 paperback

A catalogue record for this book is available
from the British Library

Printed in Hong Kong

10   9   8   7   6   5   4   3   2
03   02   01   00   99   98   97   96

KING ALFRED'S COLLEGE
WINCHESTER

0230127X   792·015
KAY

Contents

General Editor's Preface

In the past ten years, Theatre Studies has experienced remarkable international growth, students seeing in its marriage of the practical and the intellectual a creative and rewarding discipline. Some countries are now opening school and degree programmes in Theatre Studies for the first time; others are having to accommodate to the fact that a popular subject attracting large numbers of highly motivated students has to be given greater attention than hitherto. The professional theatre itself is changing, as graduates of degree and diploma programmes make their way through the 'fringe' into established theatre companies, film and television.

Two changes in attitudes have occurred as a result: first, that the relationship between teachers and practitioners has significantly improved, not least because many more people now have experience of both; secondly, that the widespread academic suspicion about theatre as a subject for study has at least been squarely faced, if not fully discredited, Yet there is still much to be done to translate the practical and educational achievements of the past decade into coherent theory, and this series is intended as a contribution to that task. Its contributors are chosen for their combination of professional and didactic skills, and are drawn from a wide range of countries, languages and styles in order to give some impression of the subject in its international perspective.

This series offers no single programme or ideology; yet all its authors have in common the sense of being in a period of transition and debate out of which the theory and practice of theatre cannot but emerge in a new form.

JULIAN HILTON

Acknowledgements

In the course of completing this book, many people have been generous with their time and interest and I have received invaluable support from institutions and funding bodies. The University of Warwick granted me a period of study leave which allowed the project to be completed. An important part of my research would not have been possible without financial support from the British Academy, the University of Warwick and the Joint School of Theatre Studies of the University of Warwick, which allowed me to undertake a period of study in New York. Here I was greatly assisted by the staff of the Museum of Modern Art, the Performing Arts Research Center, the Dance Collection and the Jerome Robbins Archive of the Recorded Moving Image of the New York Public Library at Lincoln Center. I should also like to thank those artists and other individuals whose generosity with their time, and help with source material, has been much appreciated. In particular, I should like to thank Michael Kirby, Joan Jonas, Richard Foreman, Ping Chong, Elsa Jacobson of the Brooklyn Academy of Music, Richard Schechner, George Ashley, and Bruce Allardyce of the Ping Chong Company. Finally, I should like to express my gratitude to the late John Cage for an interview of special value to this book, but which was conducted before this project was conceived.

The author and publishers wish to thank Peters Edition Ltd, London, for permission to reproduce *4'33''* and *0'00'' (4'33'' No. 2)* by John Cage.

Every effort has been made to trace all copyright holders, but if any have been inadvertently overlooked the publishers will be pleased to make the necessary arrangements at the first opportunity.

N. K.

To Diane

Introduction

Limiting the Postmodern

It would seem only reasonable to begin a book entitled *Postmodernism and Performance* by defining the term 'postmodern' and, in turn, the characteristics of 'postmodern theatre'. Any attempt to provide such an explanation, however, must consider first of all the difficulties that intrude upon any categorical definition of what the 'postmodern' actually *is*.

In *The End of Modernity* (Oxford, 1988) the philosopher Gianni Vattimo introduces the term 'postmodernity' by considering the significance of the prefix 'post-'. The condition of modernity, he argues, is dominated by the idea that the history of thought is a progressive 'enlightenment' which develops toward an ever more complete appropriation and reappropriation of its own 'foundations'.[1] Modernity, in this sense, is characterised by a consciousness of an 'overcoming' of past understandings and a striving toward future 'overcomings' in the name of a deeper recognition of that which is fundamentally legitimating and 'true', whether this is within science, the arts, morality or any other realm of thought or practice. In this context, however, the term 'postmodernity' finds itself in a peculiar position. In 'taking leave' of modernity, Vattimo argues, postmodernity is marked by a departure from the very process of overcoming that the prefix 'post-' would seem to suggest. Indeed, to use the term 'postmodernity' to indicate a literal overcoming of modernity would be to perpetuate, through a description of the postmodern, precisely that which one would define a departure from. It follows that if postmodernity indicates a 'taking leave' of this process of overcoming, then it must call into question the modernist projection forward, and so the striving toward foundation. Postmodernity, in this

1

sense, is a turning against modernity in a questioning of legitimacy which refuses to supplant that which is called into question with the *newly legitimate*.

In this context, the tensions in the term 'post-*modern*' are more easily seen. If 'postmodernity' indicates a calling into question of the modernist faith in legitimacy, then it marks modernity at its *end* rather than a true *surpassing* of modernity. It follows that one might understand 'postmodern' art and discourse as unravellings of modernist claims to legitimacy. Here the postmodern becomes complicated and multiple, occurring as phenomena which define, limit and subvert the cultural products, attitudes and assumptions of modernity. In this case the postmodern cannot be said to be properly 'free' of the modern, for the modern is the ground on which the postmodern stands, a ground with which it is in dispute and on which it is able to enter into dispute with itself. From this perspective, the problem of defining the features of a 'postmodern art' become clearer. First, in order to come to the postmodern, it seems, one must look toward the modern and the modernist.

Set against the 'critical overcoming' Vattimo describes, the various 'overturnings' of modern art can be read as struggling, through competing claim and counter-claim, towards a revelation of art's fundamental terms and values. The 'modernist work', in this sense, is one that is anxious to define itself, that overcomes the work of the recent past in a projection towards 'foundation', towards a revelation of its own unique and legitimating terms as art. It is to this process that those critics whose writing has tended to define the terms of the debate over the modernist work have looked. On precisely this basis, the American art critics Clement Greenberg and Michael Fried set out a clear and instrumental reading of the modernist work in painting and sculpture, a reading that has provided a model for influential descriptions of modern, modernist and postmodern forms of dance by the critic Sally Banes. As proponents of the modernist project, Greenberg and Fried's writing also provides a ground on which the idea of the self-legitimating work of art can be traced through the work of an earlier generation of writers on art and dance, including John Martin and Curt Sachs, as well as Suzanne Langer whose writing still shapes and influences dance theory and criticism.[2] Here, too, it becomes apparent that self-consciously 'modernist' criticism pursues the very ends that it ascribes to the 'modernist' work of art, seeking, in its address to particular works, to participate in an uncovering of the fundamental terms by which art operates.

For the critic whose sympathies lie with an unravelling of this notion of a legitimating foundation, however, a description of the postmodern in art presents a very different kind of problem. In so far as it critiques and upsets a 'modernist' striving toward foundation, the postmodern must occur as an anti-foundational disruption of precisely the move towards category and definition that a general or prescriptive account of the 'forms' and 'meanings' of postmodern art would produce. Ironically, it follows, in seeking to describe the 'postmodern' in art and performance the critic attempts to characterise that which is disruptive of categories and categorisations and which finds its identity through an evasion or disruption of conventions.

One cannot, from this perspective and with consistency, it follows, begin a study of the postmodern in performance by setting out a prescriptive view of what 'postmodern theatre' *is*. One might much more appropriately say what postmodern theatre *is not*. Evidently, this notion of the postmodern cannot readily be identified with 'conventional' theatre and drama. The forms of 'performance' considered here are 'wilfully' unconventional and 'experimental', acting, in one way or another, to upset or challenge the idea of what a painting, sculpture, dance or drama is. This 'postmodern' evasion of definition and category draws the critic, too, across disciplines and categories. Just as the idea of the modernist work and the notion of a 'postmodern style' emerge first of all in art criticism, so that 'performance' which occurs as a disruption of the projection towards the self-contained and self-supporting work of art emerges from the visual arts. Here, in addresses to exchanges, events and occurrences which disrupt the idea of the autonomous, 'auratic' work, various artists have sought to make visible 'events', occurrences and exchanges which can be considered in terms of the theatrical or the performative. In this respect, and after the modernist critic Michael Fried, this book supposes that the very idea of 'theatre' is disruptive of the 'modernist' attempt to entrench the work of art within a set of unique and exclusive terms, and that the 'postmodern' occurs as unstable, 'theatrical' and, in certain senses, 'interdisciplinary' evasions of definition and foundation.

This understanding of the postmodern also has consequences for criticism. If one accepts a 'postmodern' rejection of a final or stable foundation in art, then the 'foundation' the modernist project seeks to realise cannot be thought of as some independent thing toward which art and criticism strive. If the work of art cannot be legitimated *in its own terms*, then the very idea of the self-legitimating and self-supporting work which is in possession of its own value cannot be separated from the 'modernist' discourses of which, properly speaking, it is an effect. For the critic, this sites the 'problem' of the postmodern within criticism

itself. Like the 'modernist work', the postmodern, here, is not something 'in' art and so 'out there' as an object to which criticism responds,
but *is* an unravelling of the narrative of the modernist work, wherever
and however this occurs. The postmodern, it follows, is inseparable
from the texts and events which effect this unravelling; there is no
'authentic' or 'original' postmodernism around which various texts and
events position themselves.

In this context, and rather than attempt to survey or 'sum up' the
features of a postmodern theatre or performance, this study responds to
the 'problem of definition' which might be said to constitute the postmodern. To this end, *Postmodernism and Performance* does not offer a
definition of 'postmodern' forms and tropes, nor does it attempt a 'comprehensive' address to 'postmodern' theory or practice. Instead, the book
seeks to act in a deliberately partial way, setting out and taking issue
with readings of the postmodern in art, and of the modernist in art and
dance, in order to trace out a series of *postmodern* disruptions. Taking as
its point of departure the conflicts and exclusions produced by the model
of the 'postmodern style', which, although first formulated in architectural criticism, has formed the basis of wide-ranging descriptions of
'postmodern' departures in painting, sculpture, literature, photography,
television, film and aspects of dance and theatre, the study seeks to identify 'postmodern' instabilities with a specific notion of theatre and the
theatrical. It is in this context that the study focuses on recent and contemporary North American performance, setting limits that allow a more
effective deployment of the debts, influences and points of reference that
can be read as lying between performances, against prescriptive readings
of 'postmodern' tropes and figures. To this end the study deliberately
sets historical readings against each other so as to challenge the limits of
certain critical readings of the modern and postmodern. Finally, in
engaging with the postmodernism debate in this way, *Postmodernism
and Performance* seeks to fashion, through its own qualification and limitation of the postmodern, an appropriate address to the interdisciplinary
sources and modes of a formally diverse range of performances, an
address which could readily reach across a much broader range of work
than can possibly be considered within the confines of this book alone.

Chapter 1

From Postmodern Style to Performance

In his account of the *Strada Novissima*, an exhibition of façades designed by some 30 architects and first shown in 1980 at the Venice Biennale under the title 'The Presence of the Past', Paolo Portoghesi describes a turning against the values and stylisations of modern architecture. Including the work of Robert Stern, Ricardo Bofill, Charles Moore, Robert Venturi, John Rauch and Denise Scott Brown, Aldo Rossi, the TAU Group, Hans Hollein and Portoghesi himself, among other European and American architects, the *Strada Novissima* marked a crystallisation of a rejection of modern design which can be traced back to the late 1960s.[1] In a flat opposition to modern architecture's valorisation of uncluttered geometrical form and its casting off of reference, symbol and the traditional grammar of architecture, Portoghesi describes a new '*architecture of communication*', an 'architecture of the image',[2] characterised by ironic plays with conventions and styles from the past. Observing the loss of faith in the modernist tenets of 'useful = beautiful', 'structural truth = aesthetic prestige', ' "form follows function" ... "ornament is crime," and so on',[3] Portoghesi argues that the *Strada Novissima* speaks of a widespread attack on the modernist aspiration to a 'pure language' of form. Significantly, too, Portoghesi takes such 'postmodern' design to be more than an 'overcoming' of modernist stylisations, more than 'a simple change of direction', but 'a refusal, a rupture, a renouncement'[4] of the fundamental assumptions legitimating the modernist rejection of the past.

5

For Portoghesi this disruption of the modern has two inter-related sources; at once a loss of faith in the 'narratives' of modernity and so in the legitimacy of the 'rationalist statute' of the modernist movement and, bound up with this, the practical verification of modern buildings by their users. In his declaration of the arrival of postmodern design, *Postmodern: The Architecture of Postindustrial Society* (New York, 1982), Portoghesi suggests that modern architecture has come to be judged by its natural product:

> the modern city, the suburbs without qualities, the urban environment devoid of collective values that has become an asphalt jungle and a dormitory; the loss of local character, of connection with the place: the terrible homogulation that has made the outskirts of the cities of the whole world similar to one another, and whose inhabitants have a hard time recognizing an identity of their own.[5]

In his detailed account of *The History of Postmodern Architecture* (London, 1988), Heinrich Klotz elaborates this process, tracing, in particular, the influence of Ludwig Mies van der Rohe's rejection of 'aesthetic speculation' in favour of function through the postwar proliferation of buildings based upon his early designs. Citing Mies's sketch for an office building of 1923 as a key prototype, Klotz describes the period from the early 1950s as one in which Mies's influential dictum that architectural design should achieve 'the maximum effect with the minimum expenditure of means'[6] gained a new importance as earlier aesthetics gave way to new priorities. As a consequence, Klotz concludes, and as commercial expediency overrode many of the solutions proposed by 'classical modernism' in favour of a narrow vocabulary of cost-efficient designs, the postmodern occurs as a break with an increasingly limited and limiting vocabulary in favour of a self-conscious play with fiction, representation, symbolisation and meaning.

In his lengthy survey, *Post-modernism: The New Classicism in Art and Architecture* (London, 1987), Charles Jencks, on whom Portoghesi draws and who participated as juror and exhibitor in the *Strada Novissima*, extends this stylistic model in a consideration of the 'emergent rules' of a postmodern art. Against the overriding unity, simplicity and functionalism of modernist architecture, Jencks reads a 'postmodern' fragmentation and discord, a mode of design which abandons the ideal of the 'finished totality "where no part can be added or subtracted except for the worse" (Alberti)' in favour of a ' "difficult whole" or "frag-mented unity" '.[7] In opposition to the 'modern' aspiration to simplicity and a 'universally valid geometrical form',[8] Jencks sets a postmodern play with familiar languages and conventions which serves to disarm and disrupt particular readings of style, figure and form.

Jencks's formulation of the postmodern and the importance of his analysis becomes clearer in his description of particular pieces of work. In his account of James Stirling, Michael Wilford and Associates' *Neue Staatsgalerie, Stuttgart* (1977–84), which, he argues, is one of the 'high points' of postmodernism, and which he has presented in a number of forms,[9] Jencks sets out key aspects of the new mode of work. In a clear opposition to the modernist aspiration towards an overriding unification through style, the *Neue Staatsgalerie* is comprised not so much of a single building as 'a series of fragments placed on an acropolis (or car park)'.[10] The gallery complex embraces a variety of styles and conventions and openly sets conflicting architectural languages against each other. In this way the building fosters radically different interpretations amongst its visitors. According to Jencks:

> The young I talked to compared the building to the Pompidou Centre –
> a valid comparison only if one subtracts all the classical masonry ...
> The older people – a group of 'plein air' painters and some business-
> men – also liked the building but gave completely different readings.
> One group saw the complex as a Greco-Roman ruin, another as a typi-
> cal German institution in the tradition of Schinkel's *Altes Museum*.[11]

This 'pluralism' is produced not simply by Stirling's readiness to take up aspects of both traditional and modern styles but by his refusal to synthesise the various languages he employs or offer any uniform set of conventions. In turn the various readings which may be made of the building tend themselves be qualified and declared as 'games', for none of them can effectively resolve those conflicts Stirling has sought to heighten. It is precisely this 'pluralism' that Jencks sees as the underlying perspective of the postmodern style. Stirling's presentation of a clear, strong and unresolved dichotomy between traditionalism and modernism leads Jencks to suggest that:

> if one conclusion is drawn throughout this site it is that both posi-
> tions are legitimate and partial. Neither can win, nor can there be a
> transcendent Hegelian synthesis. There is simply the juxtaposition of
> two world views with the ironic reversal of both: the Modernist high-
> tech mode has been used for symbolic ornament, while the traditional
> rustication functions to clothe the volumes.[12]

Stirling's use of irony and paradox further qualifies this eclecticism. Jencks points to the gallery parking garage, where, having removed several blocks of masonry, Stirling allows them to fall on the ground before the building 'like ruins set in an eighteenth century landscape'.[13] The holes in the wall that these blocks reveal are, however, functional, acting as vents for the garage, while 'the fallen blocks are a sham. The sandstone and travertine of the building are only an inch thick and are suspended from a steel frame – the reality of construction today.'[14] Rather than fully take up the implications of the conventions he appropriates, Stirling transforms them through irony and juxtaposition, creating a work in which conventions are displaced, undercut and made ambiguous.

Extending his description of these 'emergent rules' through a consideration of the overlapping qualities and practices that surround this central style, Jencks goes on to catalogue the 'outbreak of parody, nostalgia and pastiche' as well as more complex means in painting and sculpture such as 'anamnesis, or suggested recollection', 'enigmatic allegory' and 'suggested narrative'[15] in work which has found a new 'complex relation to the past'.[16] Most prevalent, he argues, is a *double-coding*, use of irony, ambiguity and contradiction'[17] and he goes on to list a variety of related techniques and rhetorical figures that are important to the style, amongst them 'paradox, oxymoron, ambiguity ... disharmonious harmony, amplification, complexity and contradiction, irony, eclectic quotation, anamnesis, anastrophe, chiasmus, ellipsis, elision and erosion'.[18]

Such departures from the vocabulary and aesthetic of the dominant modes of modern architecture speak not simply of a shift of 'style' but of a new attitude towards the nature and purpose of stylisation. Evidently, for many modern architects, the move towards economy, simplicity and functionalism was underwritten by political and moral imperatives. In his 'Principles of Bauhaus Production' of 1926 Walter Gropius set the making of art against the industrial production process, calling for an architecture that, defined in strictly functional terms, would give up 'romantic gloss and wasteful frivolity'[19] in favour of a limited vocabulary of primary forms and colours. For Frank Lloyd Wright, and despite his own deviations from the modernist ideal,[20] this question of legitimacy could be addressed in purely aesthetic terms. Wright's influential call for an 'Organic Architecture' of 1911 epitomised the modernist desire for an overarching unification through style. Here, all aspects of the building, including chairs, tables, cabinets 'even musical instruments' would be 'of the building, never fixtures upon it'.[21] In the writing of Le Corbusier, in particular, the connection between this straining towards function, simplicity, a vocabulary of basic geometrical forms and a revelation of the essential and so legitimating terms of architecture becomes explicit. In *Towards a New Architecture* (London, 1927) he presents the first of three reminders to architects, in which he asserts that:

> Architecture is the masterly, correct and magnificent play of masses brought together in light. Our eyes are made to see forms in light; light and shade reveal these forms; cubes, cones, spheres, cylinders or pyramids are the great primary forms which light reveals to advantage; the image of these is distinct and tangible within us. It is for that reason that these are *beautiful forms, the most beautiful forms.*[22]

In this context, Portoghesi, Klotz and, particularly, Jencks's consideration of 'postmodern style' may be understood in terms of a falling away of the idea of a fundamental core or legitimating essence which might privilege one vocabulary over another. This loss of faith is evident in the rubrics Jencks himself compiles. Whereas modernist architecture, in striving towards its own foundation, is concerned with its own unique properties, with a purpose and presence to be, literally, imposed upon the landscape, the vocabulary of 'postmodern' architecture is concerned to put its own purpose and presence into question. The tropes Jencks lists engage in seemingly self-effacing and playful or quizzical denials of the forms and figures which they bring before the user or viewer. In these respects, this postmodernism is constituted by a playing of languages and figures against each other and through this a disarming of the very elements of which it consists.

This idea of the postmodern clearly has a resonance that goes beyond the realm of architectural practice. Extending Portoghesi and Jencks's analyses of architecture, Linda Hutcheon, in *A Poetics of Postmodernism* (London, 1988), and while privileging literature, suggests that analogous work has appeared in painting, sculpture, film, video, dance, television and music. Beginning with the notion that postmodernism is a phenomenon that at once 'uses and abuses, installs and then subverts, the very concepts it challenges',[23] Hutcheon argues that recent popular 'paradoxical' fiction has given rise to work which is specifically postmodern. In her discussion of such novels as Gabriel Garcia Marquez's *One Hundred Years of Solitude*, Gunther Grass's *The Tin Drum*, John Fowles's *A Maggot*, Nigel Williams's *Star Turn* and Salman Rushdie's *Shame*, Hutcheon focuses upon an ironic and self-conscious use of technique married to an acute awareness of historical context and process.

Here, she suggests, a genre of work arises which, in addressing the
writing of history, not only considers its own 'constructing, ordering and
selecting processes'[24] but in doing so offers self-reflexive narratives
which address their own implication and participation in the historical
processes they critique.

In Rushdie's *Shame*, for example, Hutcheon cites the narrator's open
address to his own position as 'insider/outsider' writing about the events
of Pakistan:

> *Outsider! Trespasser! You have no right to this subject!* ... I know:
> nobody ever arrested me. Nor are they ever likely to. *Poacher!*
> *Pirate! We reject your authority. We know you, with your foreign lan-*
> *guage wrapped around you like a flag: speaking about us in your*
> *forked tongue, what can you tell but lies?* I reply with more questions:
> is history to be considered the property of the participants solely? In
> what courts are such claims staked, what boundary commissions map
> out the territories?[25]

Writing in English, Rushdie addresses the process by which, in the
wake of its formation, Pakistani history was written, and so *rewritten*,
in imported tongues. In doing so, however, Rushdie implicitly
acknowledges the implication of his own writing in the processes he
critiques, forced, as he is, by the very history he recounts, to write in
England and in English. In this respect, Rushdie offers a text that
brings its own position into question, and that draws the reader towards
an awareness that its subject-matter is to be found in part through the
way it reveals itself to be enmeshed within and compromised by the
very conflicts it considers.

Other work uses a variety of analogous techniques to a similar end.
In *Foe*, J. M. Coetzee addresses the question of 'the relation of "story"
and "history" writing to "truth" and exclusion'[26] in a play on Defoe's
Robinson Crusoe. Here Coetzee supposes that Defoe derived his story
from a subsequently silenced woman and in doing so allows himself to
explore the creation of interpenetrating perspectives and fictions that
come to surround the event, including, by implication, his own. In
contrast Marquez's *One Hundred Years of Solitude* and Grass's *Tin
Drum* use parodic reference to other texts in order to put their own
authority and, by implication, the authority of any act of writing into
question, so undermining, through their own overt construction of
historical discourses, the distinctions between history and fiction.

From the early 1980s various theatre performances have emerged which can be read against these models of the postmodern. The work of Ping Chong, who collaborated closely with Meredith Monk until the late 1970s, has been read in terms analogous to the 'fragmented unity' or 'difficult whole' Jencks outlines. Jonathan Kalb describes Ping Chong's use of a 'fragmented narrative' in pieces which 'contained story elements, but [whose] purpose was not mainly to tell a story'.[27] Noel Carroll, in an article for *The Drama Review*, goes further, noting that in this multi-media work:

> each constituent medium, each channel of address is usually discreet: Chong shifts rather than mixes media. Each new medium introduces a separate issue rather than building toward a unified effect or theme ... Only gradually does one become aware of who the characters are; since only selected bits of events are represented, one grasps the outline of the underlying story slowly, while many details remain obscure.[28]

Under the direction of Elizabeth LeCompte, and beginning with the third play of their *Rhode Island Trilogy*, *Nyatt School* (1978), the Wooster Group have combined excerpts from plays with images, actions, film and sound drawn from a variety of sources to produce often disruptive and alarming performance collages. *Nyatt School* is structured around six 'examinations' of *The Cocktail Party*, each of which is set against material ranging from a recording of the play featuring Alec Guinness to reconstructions of popular comedy-horror sequences. *Point Judith* (1979) is structured around a 13 minute-long rendering of *Long Day's Journey Into Night* pared down to its most famous lines and played at high speed. *Route 1 & 9 (The Last Act)* (1981) sets extracts from Thornton Wilder's *Our Town* against reconstructed blackface routines by Pigmeat Markham as well as video and film. *L.S.D. (... Just the High Points ...)* (1984) combines a 30-minute performance of *The Crucible* with reconstructions of the performers' experiences of taking LSD and the reproduction through performance of a film record of a public debate between Dr Timothy Leary and Gordon Liddy. *Frank Dell's Temptation of St Anthony* (1987) collages, among other things, rehearsals of a stand-up routine, after Lenny Bruce, and televised interviews with naked respondents in the manner of New York's 'Channel J' with images and narrative lines drawn from Flaubert's *La Tentation de Saint Antoine*, while *Brace Up!* (1990) appropriates Chekhov's *Three Sisters*. Not only do the Wooster Group draw their material from a wide variety of sources, but in their juxtaposition of 'found' elements they resist integrating the various aspects of their presentations into a unified whole. Frequently, these conflicts are amplified by corresponding contrasts in style, heightening a sense of quotation, where texts, sequences and images are set against each other in such a way that they come to stand on uncertain and unstable ground.

In the later work of Joan Jonas, who trained as a sculptor in the early 1960s and participated in the 'post-modern' American dance of the 1960s and early 1970s, familiar narratives, genres and styles are treated in ways which seem calculated to disrupt their ability to unify a performance. *Upside Down and Backwards* (1979) is structured around a collage of retold and invented narrative lines. Beginning with recordings of her own versions of two Grimm Brothers' fairy tales, *The Frog Prince* and *The Boy Who Went Out to Learn Fear,* Jonas presents a literal paragraph-by-paragraph montage of the stories read in reverse with actions, images and descriptions that disrupt and digress from the sequence. As the piece progresses so the narratives collapse into each other, finally merging into a new, dense and fractured story. Rather than offer its audience a clear way through the piece, a central line and sequence through which meaning and significance can be clarified, Jonas's narratives are incorporated into the performance in such a way that they undercut and subvert one another.

Under the terms of this model, one might go on to consider Karen Finley's use of 'pornographic' language and imagery in monologue performances such as *The Constant State of Desire* (1986) and *We Keep Our Victims Ready* (1992) which have been accused both of subverting and confirming the abuses she would vilify as she replays them before her audiences. Finley's work might be contrasted with Laurie Anderson's appropriations and displacements of popular imagery and her telling of paradoxical stories in pieces such as *United States* (1983)[29] as well as her breaching of the conventional distinctions between fine art, video art, music video, performance art and rock performance. Both Anderson and the Wooster Group's multi-media performances can be related to Yvonne Rainer's multi-media work of the early 1970s in which a self-conscious manipulation of narrative elements serves to invite readings of character and plot while pointedly resisting any final or single coherence. Emerging out of her work with the Judson Dance Theater and The Grand Union, such pieces as *Rose Fractions* (1969) and *This is the story of a woman who ...* (1972) employ a form of 'bricolage' in which narrative development is displaced and undermined as the audience's attention is drawn from one narrative element to another, or between conflicting narrative promises. Alternatively, the Mabou Mines' *Red Horse Animation* (1972) employs a single narrative which self-consciously traces its own animation, observing and drawing attention to the coherences it variously offers and withdraws, in a subversion of narrative stability and transparency. One might go on to address Spalding Gray's treatment of monologue and persona,[30] Richard Schechner's deconstruction of texts such as *Don Juan* through game-structures and antithetical narratives and events,[31] Meredith Monk's use of imagery and story in such pieces as *Vessel* and *Education of a Girl Child* of the early 1970s or Kathy Acker's overtly intertextual texts for the theatre such as *Lulu* (1987) and *Birth of the Poet* (1985).

Against postmodern style

Despite its prolific nature, however, and especially where it is extended across the arts in this manner, the model of a 'postmodern style' raises questions concerning how one acts critically in dealing with the 'postmodern'. In drawing on an even expanded list of self-effacing or paradoxical tropes which are taken as characterising a 'postmodern art', one risks moving unself-consciously away from that which one would identify. Despite the fact that these 'postmodern' figures exemplify an attitude towards their own presence and value which seems quite opposed to the 'modernist' reaching towards foundation, the very fact of this opposition tends to effect the surpassing of one 'style' with another. Ironically, this model even sets out a stylistic paradigm of a 'postmodern' pluralism and fragmentation for which there is no 'modern' correlate precisely because of the contradictory and fragmentary nature of modernism in the arts. It follows that, despite its declaration of a new 'complex' relation to the past, this model of the postmodern risks a characteristically 'modern' shrugging off of past and present alternatives.

This exclusivity becomes particularly evident in an address to theatre and performance. The work of the Wooster Group, Ping Chong, Joan Jonas, Yvonne Rainer and others who employ a 'fragmented' style in presentations which might be read as incorporating that which they challenge in a 'postmodern' parody,[32] are closely bound to other very different kinds of presentation. The productions of Richard Foreman and Robert Wilson are evidently important to the Wooster Group's work, and can be read as elaborating distinctly 'postmodern' contingencies and fragmentations, yet neither Foreman nor Wilson's pieces exemplify a postmodern 'quotation' or 'double-coding'. In turn, both Foreman and Wilson's work can be set against various departures of performance art and dance which attack self-consciously *modernist* practices yet whose 'style', where the idea of a style can be sustained, is quite removed from the characteristics of a 'postmodern style'. As if to compound these complexities, both Joan Jonas and Yvonne Rainer's multi-media performance, and their address to narrative, developed from presentations which, in drawing explicitly on minimal art, overtly rejected a play with conventional form and figure.

In response to this, and instead of looking toward an elaboration of a 'postmodern style' through a separating out of contrasting figures and tropes or even of differing postmodern 'genres', one might more usefully acknowledge criticism's implication in the construction of the postmodern and ask questions of this model itself. Thus the tendency of this account of a 'postmodern practice' towards exclusion and prescription might be challenged through a reconsideration of two of its principal aspects; first, its dispute with the modernist claim to the work's possession of its own identity and, in this context, the 'postmodern' claim to a new and 'newly complex' relation to the past. In this way, one might set the ground for a reading of the postmodern across a more diverse range of work before returning, finally, to performances that can be linked with this attitude to 'style'.

Meaning and the postmodern

In exploring contradictions and weaknesses within Ferdinand de Saussure's account of the functioning of language, Jacques Derrida sets out an understanding of language, and of the functioning of the sign, in which meaning is never fully *present*. Set against the method and import of Derrida's analysis, the 'postmodern' dispute with foundation can be qualified both in terms of a departure from the modern and a self-reflexive turning of what would become the 'work' against the forms and figures upon which it ostensibly depends.

Saussure's structural linguistics rests upon the idea that language operates as a self-contained, self-regulating system upon which the identity and functioning of its individual elements depend. Against the understanding of language as an historically determined phenomenon consisting of an aggregate of elements and rules which have 'acquired' meanings, Saussure sets out a description of language as a system always complete in itself and which functions independently of its historical aspect. Key to this is his distinction between the two aspects of any linguistic system; between *parole* and *langue*. Language, Saussure argues, is always manifested as parole, as a specific use of particular elements, and yet this use is always dependent upon the langue, the set of rules and relationships which constitute the system of language and whose existence is implicit in any use of any of its elements. Through this relationship, Saussure re-reads an earlier understanding of the constitution of the sign. Conventionally, a sign can be understood to consist of two aspects: a signifier (a sound, mark, movement and so on) and a signified (a concept or unit of meaning). It is through the joining of signifier and signified that the sign comes into being and presents itself as meaningful. By drawing this reading into the context of the functioning of parole and langue Saussure is able to argue that the relationship between a particular signifier and signified is not determined by any 'fitness' of one to the other, but is purely a function of the self-contained structure of language itself.

Saussure's argument leads to two radical conclusions concerning the operation of language. In the first place, if the joining of a signifier to a signified is purely a function of a conventional and self-contained structure, it follows that the referent, or that to which the sign refers, does not play a part in the production of meaning. As a self-contained system, the functioning of language is not dependent upon anything beyond its own terms. Indeed, Saussure takes language itself to be the pre-condition to thought and so to any knowledge of that to which language may refer. In this context, the full implication of the conventional nature of language for the functioning of the signifier becomes clearer. If the joining of a particular signifier to a particular signified is determined only by the arbitrary relationships which make up the language system, then the ability of a signifier to join with a signified is at each moment dependent upon the signifier's relationship to all the other elements of which the system consists. In practice, as Saussure points out, this means that the reading of a signifier literally involves, at the moment of reading, the elimination of all other possibilities which the structure holds. It follows that meaning, in the shape of the signified, is not brought into play by what the signifier *is*, not by any positive value or quality it *possesses*, but only by the set of differences and so oppositions out of which the particular structure is made up.

One can, however, and after Derrida, set the very self-contained nature of this system against itself. By supposing that the signifier functions through its difference from other signifiers, and yet that through this difference the signifier is able to join with a signified, Saussure can be accused of supposing that there is a realm of the signified, and so of meaning, somehow existing beyond the functioning of the signifier.

Meaning exists beyond the signs.

Only by gaining access to such a realm can the play of *difference*, by which the signifier functions, result in the *presence* of meaning. Plainly, though, any such realm would both precede and exist beyond language as Saussure describes it, for neither the signifier nor the signified can have an independent existence. It would follow from this that the very set of oppositions which serve, in Saussure's system, to make the sign meaningful, cannot in themselves allow meaning to become *present*.

To put this system into question in this way, however, is to doubt the very 'decidability' of meaning. Within Saussure's conception of language, the ability of the signifier to make a relationship with the signified is dependent not upon what the signifier *is* but upon what it *is not*. Signification, then, is a function not of presence but of absence and difference, for the signifier functions only with reference to all those possibilities the system holds and which it is differentiated from. It follows that where the signifier is cut off from the anchor of an independent signified, where the unit of meaning becomes inseparable from the functioning of the signifier, then, paradoxically, meaning becomes subject to the same processes of differentiation which permit the functioning of the signifier. Thus, meaning is always being defined not simply in terms of what it *is* but in terms of *what it is not*. Here, it follows, where 'the signified always already functions as signifier',[33] the sign can never be self-identical, never fully in possession of 'meaning', for the move toward the signified finds itself caught in the endless reference between signifiers, and so a reading which is beyond closure.

This disjoining not only of the sign from the referent but of the signifier from the independent signified has profound consequences. In deconstructing the 'transcendental signified', Derrida acts on the assumption that, as an effect of the uncertain and undecidable play of signifiers, the signified is always subject to the play of difference and deferral within any linguistic system, always subject to a 'differance'.[34] Importantly, too, Derrida does not 'overcome' Saussure in the name of another foundational account of the operation of language and the functioning of meaning, but acts in such a way as to inhabit Saussure's terms while calling them into question. Through such criticism, Derrida challenges by his very means fundamental assumptions of criticism and philosophy, acting to subvert claims to the transparency of language and the possibility of uncontested meaning by deploying the contradictions texts suppress, and which are the result of this very slippage, against themselves.

After Derrida's proposition, then, and in terms of the work of art, the modernist projection towards foundation can be read as an attempt to overcome the arbitrariness and instability of the sign.[35] In striving toward 'essence' the modernist work seeks to realise qualities and values which are legitimate *in their own terms*, and so to transcend the play of difference Derrida reveals in an appeal to the 'transcendental signified' and so the *presence* of meaning. The postmodern disruption of this modernism, it follows, would occur as a disruption of the illusion of the self-identical and unitary sign, and so as an uncovering of the uncertain and indefinite play between elements the modernist projection towards foundation attempts to suppress. Consistently with this, however, one must conclude that the figures or terms out of which the 'postmodern work' is constituted cannot properly be said to be in *possession* of its 'meanings', for here the postmodern occurs as a disruption of this very claim to meaning.

Equally, and on this basis, one might go on to extend a reading of the postmodern through the disjoining of the signifier from the signified and in doing so question the idea that the postmodern rests upon or defines itself in relation to the modern. Here, the postmodern would entail a giving over of the modernist concern for singularity, depth and the stability of meaning to a free play of signifiers, to exhibitions of fragmentation and multiplicity, where meaning is shifting and undecidable. For Jean Baudrillard, this reconsideration of the functioning of the sign leads to a conflation of the signifier and the referent through which the operation of contemporary signifying systems may be read. In an echo of the postmodern style's play with codes, Baudrillard takes the contemporary condition to be that of the simulacrum, the material imitation, the copy without an original, the 'hyperreal'; a condition without 'transcendence or depth'[36] and marked by an endless parade and exchange of equivalences.

In both these cases, the corollary of the postmodern disruption of the modernist claim to foundation is that the postmodern cannot, with consistency, be defined in terms of a given set of formal elements without a reversion to the modernist claim that meaning (and so the signified) resides 'within' and so is 'present to' the work of art *in its own terms*. One can conclude here, then, that the postmodern cannot be identified with particular figures or forms precisely because the 'postmodern' occurs as a displacement and subversion of the very terms of which it would seem to consist.

While such a reconsideration of the functioning of the sign permits a thinking of the postmodern in terms of a declaration of the undecidability of meaning, Jean-François Lyotard's understanding of the contingent nature of language-systems allows an extension of this formulation in terms of narrative and narrativity. In *The Postmodern Condition: A Report on Knowledge* (Manchester, 1984), Lyotard reads the 'critical overcoming' through which the 'modern' reaches toward foundation in terms of the conflict between differing systems of knowledge. The modern, here, involves an act of 'totalization', an appeal to 'metanarrative', to a story that can explain the true meaning of all other stories. Conversely, the postmodern occurs as an awareness of the contingent nature of systems of knowledge. Thus, Lyotard suggests:

> I will use the term *modern* to designate any science that legitimates itself with reference to a metadiscourse ... making an explicit appeal to some grand narrative, such as the dialectics of the Spirit, the hermeneutics of meaning, the emancipation of the rational or working subject, or the creation of wealth.[37]

While:

> Simplifying to the extreme, I define *postmodern* as incredulity toward metanarratives.[38]

Lyotard's distinction rests upon the idea that all knowledge, including scientific knowledge, ultimately draws its legitimacy from agreements made by participants in a language-game, agreements constructed and perpetuated through the process by which knowledge is imparted and received. In this sense all knowledge is narrative knowledge, for all knowledge depends for its legitimacy upon values and beliefs constructed and confirmed by a process of telling, and so an active relationship between addressor and addressee. In this context, Lyotard takes narrative to have two aspects: *figure*, the event of narrativity, or the telling, and *discourse*, the process by which narrative represents and gives meaning. The modern, in its appeal to metanarrative, it follows, suppresses the event of its own narrativity, emphasising *discourse* over *figure*. Conversely, the postmodern is marked by an awareness of the event of narrativity; the contingent aspect of narrative that is so completely *other* to discourse that it cannot be incorporated, accounted for or 'totalized' by it. Here the 'postmodern' indicates a moment of struggle between narratives, or systems of knowledge, in which the awareness of *figure* disrupts the claim of *discourse* to universality. The postmodern occurs as a moment in which 'no single instance of narrative can exert a claim to dominate narratives by standing beyond it';[39] where the 'grand narrative' is given over to the 'little narrative' and the telling of *the* story is displaced by the telling of *a* story that looks toward its own displacement. Lyotard's account of 'postmodern art' extends these terms. Here the postmodern cannot be described as a stable category for it occurs as a breaking down or evasion of categories, a radical scepticism towards and transgression of that which is *known*. For Lyotard, this idea of the postmodern as an instability undermines the commonsense view that the postmodern is that which follows the modern. In 'Answering the Question: What is Postmodernism?', he asserts that 'a work can become modern only if it is first postmodern. Postmodernism ... is not modernism at its end but in its nascent state, and this state is constant.'[40] Taken as a moment in which the terms in play are disrupted, as a profoundly disruptive breaking of rules, the postmodern in art becomes deeply implicated within the formulation of the modern as 'a tradition against itself'.[41] On being asked what art might be considered postmodern, Lyotard responds:

All that has been received, if only yesterday ... must be suspected. What space does Cezanne challenge? The Impressionists'. What object do Picasso and Braque attack? Cezanne's. What presupposition does Duchamp break with in 1912? That which says one must make a painting, be it cubist. And Buren questions that other presupposition which he believes had survived untouched by the work of Duchamp: the place of presentation in the work.[42]

In this sense, the term 'postmodern art' is a contradictory formulation, describing an occurrence which at once refers to and escapes from the languages by which it is recognised. Postmodern art is, ironically from the critic's point of view, an occurrence beyond categories; it is that which, in Bill Readings reading of Lyotard, 'both is and is not art at the same time'.[43] Such notions exemplify the postmodern as an instability, as an evasion, a making visible of uncertainties or contingencies. In making such an equation, these readings implicate the postmodern 'event' in that which it precedes and surrounds, looking towards the possibility of its future transformation, and so of the recurrence of the modern.

Here, again, the postmodern is resistant to prescription and exclusivity. Occurring as a crisis forced into being by a breaking of rules or a reversal of terms, the 'postmodern' indicates a calling into question of the languages, styles and figures through which it is seen. Against this, one could set Jencks's and Hutcheon's accounts of treatments of styles and discourses, such as 'traditionalism and modernism', 'history and fiction', in such a way that the conventional oppositions through which they secure their identity and efficacy are called into question. In this way, the very ground on which the 'work' depends is rendered unstable, as the languages by which it is constituted are deployed in such a way as to make visible problems and limitations which cannot be resolved or transcended. This 'postmodernism' is synonymous with a kind of *excess*; an event or events produced by a clash or subversion of the rules, terms and conventions out of which the work would be constituted. It follows that the postmodern in art is subversive and transgressive, that it occurs as a critical and sceptical stepping beyond bounds, a disruption that purposefully upsets the terms by which the 'work of art' would constitute itself.

History and the postmodern

This qualification of the postmodern also puts into question the nature of the new and 'newly complex' address to the past with which the 'postmodern style' is often identified. If language is a site of conflict between discourses which act to construct values and perspectives without *a priori* claim to truth, then the writing of history must be subject to the struggle between narratives. It follows from this that the past cannot simply be considered to be 'out there', as a thing which is somehow 'available', but must be read as an effect of the very narratives that would seek to describe it. Here, language itself must be seen as limiting and shaping any view of history, while the historical narrative must be understood as rooted in and acting to legitimate contemporary forms, assumptions and ideas.

It follows from this, though, that the 'postmodern' address to 'historical' material should be identified with a loss of faith in the efficacy of the very historical and theoretical models that legitimate the modern 'overcoming' of the past. Perversely, while the 'modernist' project rejects the past precisely *because* it can be read, understood and so transcended, the postmodern self-consciously 'replays' images of a past that cannot be known, but that can only be constructed and reconstructed through a play of entirely contemporary references to the *idea* of the past.

This upsetting of the writing of history not only has consequences for an understanding of the 'postmodern' 'presence of the past' but to a reading of the history of the postmodern itself. Here, where the distinctions between history, theory, criticism and fiction become blurred as each is seen to be a discourse which creates the 'object' it would address, the perspicacity of all theory and discourse is threatened. In this context, Baudrillard understands the very idea of the 'object' of criticism to be a product of the desire for the definitively *meaningful*; a desire, it would follow, that is played out most fully through the modernist projection toward foundation. In *The Ecstasy of Communication* he argues:

> The critique of objects was based on signs saturated with meaning, along with their phantasies and unconscious logic as well as their prestigious differential logic. Behind this dual logic lies the anthro-pological dream: the realm of the object existing beyond and above exchange and use, above and beyond equivalence ... [44]

It follows from this that a history of the development of a 'postmod-ern style' cannot be accepted as a 'true' explanation of how a store of figures and styles from the past became newly available to contemporary artists, for such a history effects a 'backward glance'[45] which acts to construct the very notion of the postmodern style it seeks to describe.

With these qualifications in mind, and instead of attempting to con-struct a single history, one might come to consider the postmodern in terms of the interaction of different histories and the various descriptions of the modern and the postmodern which they construct. Thus Jencks's account of a 'progression' of styles toward a 'full-blown' postmodern-ism might be set against Umberto Eco's description of the avant-garde's destruction of itself through its attempt to 'deface the past'. Eco's account is, in fact, analogous to Jencks's, reading the postmodern in terms of an ironic quotation of familiar elements. Yet in using the figure of a self-destruction rather than a progression forward, Eco draws dif-ferent meanings around these tropes. Rather than suppose that the post-modern's 'return to the past' promises a 'new classicism', Eco traces a process by which the impossibility of its erasure leads to an ironic atti-tude towards the act of remembering. Since the past cannot be destroyed, he suggests, 'because its destruction leads to silence', it 'must be revisited: but with irony, not innocently'.[46]

Alternatively, that work which would seem to undermine the legitimacy of the self-contained work of art might be set against the modernist projection towards an autonomous aesthetic sphere and an absolute distinction between the respective arts. In *Sociology of Post-modernism* (London, 1990), Scott Lash, associating non-realist and anti-realist modernist painting with the differentiation of the aesthetic sphere from the political and the social, describes the postmodern in terms of a de-differentiation, a 'transgression of the boundaries that separates the aesthetic from other cultural spheres'.[47] In the work of art this de-differentiation takes the form of an explicit transgression and confusion of category, a 'postmodernist refusal to separate the author from his or her work or the audience from the performance'.[48]

More radically, but reflecting the same process in an extension of Lyotard's description of the postmodern, Thomas Docherty, in *After Theory: Post-modernism/Post-Marxism* (London, 1990), offers an account of art and criticism in the 'wake' of theory. In this context, the 'postmodern work' emerges as an evasion of categories, occurring not so much as a 'thing', as a 'rootless movement'; a work or act of writing existing in paradoxical or transgressive forms and in a perpetual and anti-foundational flight from itself. Here, ironically, postmodern strategies share the modern preoccupation with the rules and forms of art, yet in the event of the postmodern these rules are sought out not in the name of an essence but in an attempt to evade the realisation of a self-legitimating narrative. The postmodern in art, then, takes on the nascent state Lyotard ascribes to the postmodern condition, seeking always to postpone the possibility of the 'modern' and so its own final definition.

Performance and the postmodern

If the postmodern occurs as a disruption of a striving toward foundation, as an unravelling of the *meaningful*, then one cannot prescribe the features of a 'postmodern art' either according to its 'meanings' or the features which might 'best' represent it. Similarly, if one cannot have access to a history of the postmodern, one cannot impartially limit the forms of the postmodern through a definition of the history and purposes of the modern. Indeed, here and in both these respects, the postmodern occurs as an unravelling of precisely such definitions and limits through its own dispute with foundation. At the same time, though, this notion of what one *cannot* say looks toward a certain kind of circumscription of the postmodern in art.

If, as Linda Hutcheon suggests, parody might be considered 'a perfect postmodern form', then perhaps performance may be thought of as a primary postmodern mode. Where the postmodern in art, literature and performance is identified with a disruption, with instabilities precipitated by a challenge to the 'totalising' capacity of the terms in play, then the postmodern might be best conceived of as something that *happens*. Here, Hutcheon's 'parody' may itself be understood as giving rise to an 'event', an instability forced into being by a strategy or figure which challenges and upsets its own definition. Critically, too, this idea of an 'occurrence', of the postmodern as something that 'happens', allows a formulation of the 'postmodern event' which breaks free from specific forms and figures. Such a postmodern 'theatricality' does not supersede Hutcheon's notion of a postmodern parody, or Jencks's 'double-coding', but coexists with it, as a moment *produced* by it. 'Theatricality', in this sense, is not some*thing*, but is an effect, and an ephemeral one at that. It is in terms of this instability, of this *excess* produced by the figures in play, that one might then speak of a moment which is both 'theatrical' or 'performative' and properly *postmodern*.

In this context, the condition of 'performance' may be read, in itself, as tending to foster or look towards postmodern contingencies and instabilities. More than any other mode of work, one might argue, a 'performance' vacillates between presence and absence, between displacement and reinstatement. It is for precisely these reasons that both theatre and the condition of theatricality have been read as peculiarly resistant to the modernist project and even as necessarily effecting a corruption of the modernist ideal.[49]

At the same time, though, this very reading of the postmodern throws into question the oppositions such a privileging of medium and form would rest upon. Plainly, this 'postmodern' moment is not the property of any particular discipline. The work addressed within the parameters of this study, alone, emerges variously in a reconceiving of the 'object' in art, in the extension of this conception of the 'object' into theatre-presentations, in an unravelling, through dance, of a modernist projection beyond performance's ephemerality and contingency, and, finally, and after the postmodern style, in subversions of and clashes between narrative elements. In so far as they 'are' postmodern, these presentations are disruptive and evasive, occurring as questionings of limits and boundaries, as threats, even, to the terms by which they themselves invite definition. The postmodern in art and performance, here, occurs as a making visible of contingencies or instabilities, as a fostering of differences and disagreements, as transgressions of that upon which the promise of the work itself depends and so a disruption of the move toward containment and stability.

Chapter 2

Theatricality and the Corruption of the Modernist Work

In identifying the postmodern in art with a disruption of the move toward self-containment and self-sufficiency, one can readily set a 'postmodern' play with appropriated figures and forms against very different kinds of presentation.

Despite what would seem to be a complete removal from the 'conventional' vocabulary of theatre and a 'postmodern' eclecticism, the minimal art of the late 1960s was not only a touchstone for Michael Fried's seminal defence of the modernist project, but also for a wide variety of entries into theatre and performance. For Richard Foreman, Michael Kirby and Robert Wilson, as well as the Body Artist Vito Acconci and performance artists such as Joan Jonas, minimalism and minimal art would seem to have offered a direct intersection between art and theatre. The critical and aesthetic vocabulary of minimalism also provided a means by which dancers such as Yvonne Rainer could more effectively define their rejection of the dominant modes of American modern dance, while artists such as Robert Morris, whose work was influential in defining a minimalist aesthetic, readily stepped into dance and performance.[1] In this context, minimalism provides a meeting between a critical defence of the modernist work which explicitly opposes 'theatricality' in art, and a range of performance practices and interactions between art and theatre which challenge the ideal of the self-contained and self-determining work of art.

24

Theatricality and the modernist work

For Clement Greenberg, the influential theorist and proponent of American modernism, the emergence of American abstract painting after the war continued the self-critical development of a specifically modernist art. Arguing that major art 'is impossible, or almost so, without a thorough assimilation of the major preceding period or periods',[2] Greenberg stressed the inheritance from European painters and understood both Abstract Expressionism and the formalist painting that followed it to be firmly located within a clearly defined and progressive artistic modernism. In his seminal essay of 1962, 'After Abstract Expressionism', in which he traced this process at work, he suggests:

> The aim of the self-criticism, which is entirely empirical and not at all an affair of theory, is to determine the irreducible working essence of art and the separate arts. Under the testing of modernism more and more of the conventions of the art of painting have shown themselves to be dispensable, unessential.[3]

For Greenberg, while the work of painters such as Ashille Gorky, Willem de Kooning and Jackson Pollock of the 1940s and 1950s had continued the move toward the discovery of painting's 'viable essence',[4] making 'explicit certain constant factors of pictorial art that the past left implicit',[5] the 'cooler' formalist abstractions of the late 1950s and 1960s extended this process again and in especially significant ways. In rejecting Abstract Expressionism, painters such as Kenneth Noland, Clyfford Still, Mark Rothko, Barnett Newman, Morris Louis and Jules Olitski had, he suggested, 'established ... that the irreducible essence of pictorial art consists in but two constitutive conventions or norms: flatness and the delimitation of flatness'.[6]

Greenberg's notion of modernism in art as the culmination of an historical development with its roots in the Enlightenment not only defines an autonomy as essential to the modernist work but sees a separation between the arts as fundamental to each discipline's realisation of itself. In response to the loss of purpose that the Enlightenment secularisation brought with it, Greenberg argued, the arts could either become a mere entertainment or attempt to demonstrate and clarify the uniqueness of each art and the experience it could offer. It follows, he suggested in his article on 'Modernist Painting' of 1965, that the 'task of self-criticism became to eliminate from the effects of each art any and every effect that might conceivably be borrowed from or by the medium of any other art'.[7]

In modernist art, then, this pursuit of the essential properties of each form becomes self-conscious and as such it is the culmination of this process. Rather than subordinate their own properties to any re-presentational end, the modernist arts attempt to address explicitly the nature of their own condition, using 'the characteristic methods of a dis-cipline to criticise the discipline itself – not in order to subvert it, but to entrench it more firmly in its area of competence'.[8] Thus modernist painting progresses toward a self-conscious focus on 'flatness, two-dimensionality'.[9] In this way each art projects itself toward its own formal essence, the discovery of those unique terms which define it as what it is. In an earlier and signal essay, 'Avant-Garde and Kitsch' of 1939, Greenberg explicitly described this process of purification as a projection toward the absolute:

> It has been in search of the absolute that the avant-garde has arrived at 'abstract' or 'nonobjective' art – and poetry, too. The avant-garde poet or artist tries in effect to imitate God by creating something valid solely on its own terms ... something *given*, increate, independent of meanings, similars or originals. Content is to be dissolved so com-pletely into form that the work of art or literature cannot be reduced in whole or in part to anything not itself.[10]

It follows that for Greenberg modernist art only makes explicit what has been the real project of art since the Enlightenment and what are the actual terms by which art has always operated. In revealing what is essential to the making and experiencing of art, he concludes, modern-ism does not lower the standing of Leonardo, Raphael, Titian, Rubens, Rembrandt or Watteau, but rather, 'What Modernism has made clear is that, though the past did appreciate masters like these justly, it often gave wrong or irrelevant reasons for doing so.'[11]

In his celebrated article 'Art and Objecthood' of 1967, the American critic Michael Fried extended the terms of Greenberg's argument in an opposition to those forms of work which would undermine or corrupt this reaching towards foundation. Attacking the minimalist sculpture, which by the mid-1960s was offering its own particular response to the 'cool' abstractions of the non-objective painters, Fried set the self-contained purity of modernist work against that which looked beyond its own terms and towards the 'literal' conditions in which an object stands. For Fried, such conditions were the most banal aspects of the object's life, and facts that any work of art must necessarily strive to suspend or defeat.

Typically, the 'minimalist' objects presented by artists such as Robert Morris, Frank Stella and Donald Judd from around 1965 and 1966 rejected not only representation, reference and symbol, but the very idea that the art-object should be composed of inter-related parts. These forms are minimal firstly in the sense that they consist of simple self-sufficient, geometrical shapes, often rectangles or cubes presented singly or in series. Placed flatly within the gallery space, such objects seem to offer themselves as irreducible 'facts', asserting nothing more than their own sheer physical presence. Yet despite their apparent pursuit of the absolute, self-supporting and self-contained work, the very 'blankness' of such objects may force a reconsideration of their actual subject-matter. For the Body Artist Vito Acconci, far from asserting their autonomy, the refusal of such sculpture to allow itself to be 'read' served to reveal to the viewer the circumstances and relationships upon which the work of art is dependent. Minimalism, he notes:

> was the art that made it necessary to recognise the space you were in. Up until that time I had probably assumed the notion of a frame. I would look at what was inside the frame, I would ignore the wall around it. Finally, then, with minimal art, I had to recognise I was in a certain floor ... I was in a certain condition, I had a headache, for example. I had a certain history, I had a certain bias ... what minimal art did for me was to confirm for myself the fact that art obviously had to be this relation between whatever it was that started off the art and the viewer.[12]

To Fried, far from revealing what is of inherent value within sculptural form, such work forces the viewer to look towards extraneous terms and relationships. While modernist composition attempts to suspend its own, literal 'objecthood' in favour of that which is essential to the interior life of the work, such objects emphasise the terms and relationships that constitute this very sense of objecthood. In resisting a reading of internal relationships between parts, in echoing the geometry of the rooms in which they are placed, and so in forcing the viewer's attention back on itself, Fried argued, the work becomes 'theatrical' and so fundamentally flawed:

> Literalist sensibility is theatrical because, to begin with, it is concerned with the actual circumstances in which the beholder encounters literalist work ... Whereas in previous art 'what is to be had from the work is located strictly within (it),' the experience of literalist art

is of an object *in a situation* – one that, virtually by definition, *includes the beholder* ... .[13]

Like theatre, too, and unlike the modernist work of art, the experience the literalist object has to offer necessarily emphasises duration. Dependent upon the developing self-consciousness of the viewer as she is drawn toward her own presence and condition before the object, the minimalist object provokes a heightened awareness of the time spent before it, the time given to it. The self-contained modernist work, however, attempts to lift itself out of even this aspect of its literal condition by offering a work which is fixed and whole, which is 'at every moment ... wholly manifest'[14] and so which may offer an experience which is complete even in the briefest of moments.

It follows that for Fried, literalist art does not represent simply a new and less-worthy departure within abstract art but an attack upon the fundamental values that legitimise art and which the modernist work seeks to make explicit. Where, after Greenberg, the arts must look to their respective essences in order to establish their uniqueness and so value, that work which insists on looking beyond these terms to a relationship with the viewer in space and time must be antithetical to the very development of art. So, Fried argues, 'there is a war going on between theatre and modernist painting, between the theatrical and the pictorial'[15] and he states categorically that '*Art degenerates as it approaches the condition of theatre*'.[16]

Nor does this theatricality emerge simply through an attention to the literal conditions in which the art-object stands. Again, following Greenberg, Fried sees the exploration of connections between the arts as a dangerous and corrupting distraction from the search for values inherent within the respective arts. He concludes:

> The concepts of quality and value – and to the extent that these are central to art, the concept of art itself – are meaningful, or wholly meaningful, only *within* the individual arts. What lies *between* the arts is theatre.[17]

Against the modernist object

In retrospect, Fried's attack upon the theatrical in art provides a framework through which earlier departures from the 'self-contained' artwork may be clearly seen. In the 1950s work by Robert Rauschenberg and Jasper Johns, who drew self-consciously on the prewar European avant-garde, signalled a rapid proliferation of forms and practices that drew attention to the presence and activity of the viewer before the painting or sculpture. In certain forms these presentations even pursued the dissolution of the physical object and a direct step into performance.

In his *White Paintings* of 1951 and 1952, Robert Rauschenberg placed the formal parameters and integrity of the work of art directly into question. Consisting of apparently 'blank' single and tryptich canvases, these presentations invite a confusion between the self-contained abstraction of a white painting and a frame which will admit elements entirely contingent upon the circumstances of their exhibition. The early showing of the pieces, lit so that the viewers' shadows were cast on to the canvas, made this explicit, while Rauschenberg has described such work as a form of 'open composition' which he sees as 'responding to the activity within their reach'.[18] Rauschenberg's later 'combines', a radical form of collage made up of disjointed and profuse collections of personal bric-a-brac, found objects and blank reproductions of familiar images and fragments of newspaper, reflect this concern to draw attention to the viewer's presence and condition before the object, threatening, by their resistance to thematic closure, to provoke an awareness of the dependency of the work upon the choices of the viewer. In this context, Rauschenberg also incorporated entirely direct references to the conditions within which the object stands. In commenting on his inclusion of working radios in combine pieces he emphasises that 'listening happens in time – looking also has to happen in time'.[19]

Like Rauschenberg, Jasper Johns's early work sought a ground on which the terms of the self-contained work might be put into question. Pursuing a deliberately limited vocabulary, in which numbers, flags and targets predominate, Johns's paintings set out formal and thematic ironies by presenting figures that resist being transformed by their incorporation into a painting. Such figures, Clement Greenberg suggests in 'After Abstract Expressionism', introduce a play between the image and its representation, offering 'the literary irony that results from *representing* flat and artificial configurations that can only be *reproduced*'.[20] Johns's appropriations are of elements that pointedly retain an aspect of their own identity, that, in one way or another, stand independently of the 'work' despite their incorporation within it. Such elements live a double life, putting the integrity of the painting into question by resisting a final closure, a complete assimilation into its formal strictures and coherences. Here Johns works to place the language and status of the painting into question and looks towards an uncertain relationship between viewer and object. In this context, the work also makes explicit addresses to the viewer's presence and activity. In _Tango_ (1955), a small music box is incorporated into a large blue canvas. While in the top left hand corner the word TANGO is printed, at the bottom of the painting, on the right, a small key protrudes through the canvas which when wound plays a hidden music box. Through these means the piece provokes an awareness of the viewer's active presence over time before the object:

> I wanted to suggest a physical relationship to the pictures that was active ... In 'Tango,' to wind the key and hear the sound, you had to stand relatively close to the painting, too close to see the outside shape of the picture.[21]

Like Rauschenberg's combines, such 'paintings' proceed on the basis that it is not simply the formal integrity of the painted surface that legitimates the work. In provoking and naming an active response, a 'dancing', _Tango_ challenges the conventional terms and parameters of painting, revealing the painting's 'objecthood' in order to force a reconsideration of the terms by which it is defined.

In his seminal essay, _Assemblages, Environments and Happenings_ (New York, 1966), Allan Kaprow traces connections between 'combine' and 'assemblage' and his own 'Happenings'. Observing the consequences of the extension of collage-sculpture, such as Rauschenberg's, into 'environmental' presentations, Kaprow suggested that where the compositional principle underlying assemblage was allowed a free development, the very idea of a compositional whole would be put into question. Not only were such environments by Claes Oldenburg, Robert Whitman, Jim Dine, Kaprow and others created without regard to the formal unities of an 'organic whole', but they refused to offer the viewer even a perceivable whole. In the generation of such work, Kaprow argues:

> Molecule-like, the material (including paint) at one's disposal grow in any desired direction and take on any shape whatsoever. In the freest of these works the field, therefore, is created as one goes along, rather than being there _a priori_, as in the case of a canvas of certain dimensions. It is a process, and one that works from the inside-out, though this should be considered merely metaphorical, rather than descriptive, since there actually exists no inside, a bounded area being necesssary to establish a field.[22]

The viewer's experience of such a 'work' is by a literal entry into its form, an entry which, while eminently theatrical in Fried's sense, also looks toward a further contingency and ephemerality. Here, Kaprow notes, the very movement and interaction of visitors within the environment sets the ground for an increasing intersection between the viewer's presence and that which the environment offers. As a result of this intersection and the contingencies it reveals, Kaprow observes:

> mechanical moving parts could be added, and parts of the created surroundings could then be rearranged like furniture at the artist's and visitor's discretion. And, logically, since the visitor could and did speak, sound and speech, mechanical and recorded, were also soon to be in order. Odours followed.[23]

The fact of many environments' impermanence, built as temporary transformations of gallery rooms, also permitted the entry of a new range of materials which escaped the conventional values and hierarchies of sculptural form. So Kaprow points to the use of debris, waste products and materials which will rapidly decay such as toilet paper and bread. Such materials, by their very presence, introduce a process of change, of 'event' into the environment. That such processes of change should be incorporated into what would be the work, Kaprow argues, 'suggests a form principle for an art which is never finished, whose parts are detachable, alterable, and rearrangeable in theoretically large numbers of ways without in the least harming the work. Indeed, such changes actually fulfil the arts' function.'[24] Such means and materials explicitly put the parameters of the work into question, divorcing a definition of what is and is not proper to the 'work of art' not only from the bounded field but even the physical integrity of the object and its elements.

While Kaprow's work takes the form of an extended and expanded collage, George Brecht, whose activities were closely bound up with the concerts, publications and events presented by the Fluxus[25] group of artists from 1961, offered games and loose assemblages of often rearrangeable objects or even unsigned objects presented variously within and outside of the formal circumstances of the gallery. His first exhibition, *toward EVENTS: an arrangement* at the Reuben Gallery, New York, in 1959, included *The Case*, a collection of small and ordinary 'found' objects whose presentation is described by Brecht in the invitation to the exhibition. Brecht's statement typifies his attitude toward his work and its containment:

THE CASE is found on a table. It is approached by one to several people and opened. The contents are removed and used in various ways
appropriate to their nature. The case is repacked and closed. The
event (which lasts possibly 10–30 minutes) comprises all sensible
occurrences between approach and abandonment of the case.[26]

The Case, like so many of the later Fluxus objects and editions, deliberately confuses the 'art-object' with its use, breaking down the conventional distinctions between the 'work' and the occasion of the viewer's
meeting with it. Here, as with so many of Brecht's presentations, the
simple re-presentation of familiar, everyday objects with little or no
transformation places the meaning, formal identity and parameters of
what would be 'the work' into question.

Prefiguring Pop Art's appropriation of the commercial image and
object and extending the environment's conflation of object and place,
Claes Oldenburg's *Store* of 1961 consisted of a real store at 107 East
2nd Street, New York. Here he kept a stock of approximately 120
everyday objects of all kinds recast in a variety of materials and offered
for sale. Oldenburg's treatment of ' "real" place' as if it were 'itself an
object'[27] threatens to collapse the boundaries between the work and its
literal context, and so between the environment and the activities within
it. In turn, the particular choice of a store also moves to conflate the
viewer with the consumer, artist with salesman, and 'art-work' with
commercial product. *The Store* might be best considered as an 'event'
not simply because of the 'performances' it might embrace, but in its
setting of conflicting meanings against each other, as objects and roles
are torn between the two aspects of the place Oldenburg directs attention toward. Here, the formal distinction between what is and is not
'proper' to the work becomes, like the meanings of the objects and
interactions Oldenburg calls attention towards, slippery and evasive of a
final determination. Indeed, the point of *The Store* seems to lie not so
much in what it *is*, but in its blocking together of conflicting readings
and possibilities.

In these contexts the emergence of strategies which look specifically
toward *performance* can be read as a final move towards an unravelling
of the discrete or bounded 'work of art'. In October 1959 Allan Kaprow
presented *18 Happenings in 6 Parts* at the Reuben Gallery in New
York,[28] in which he drew on John Cage's Black Mountain College
'event' of 1952 which had brought together a radical rethinking of
musical composition with dance by Merce Cunningham, paintings by
Rauschenberg and poetry by Charles Olsen and Mary Caroline

Richards.[29] Within a week of *18 Happenings in 6 Parts*, the Reuben Gallery showed Brecht's *toward Events: an arrangement* and, in January 1960, followed this with four days of performances by Allan Kaprow, Robert Whitman and Red Grooms. During February and March 1960, the Gallery at the Judson Church on Washington Square hosted *The Ray Gun Specs*, which presented live work by Claes Oldenburg, Jim Dine, Al Hansen, Allan Kaprow, Robert Whitman, Red Grooms and Dick Higgins.

Minimalism and the event of the work

Set against this history, both minimalism and Fried's defence of the modernist work need to be reconsidered.

Evidently, Fried's concern with minimalism is not simply that it toys with theatricality in the manner of much painting and sculpture that precedes it, but that it does so by siting itself in relation to the modernist reduction of the work to its formal essence. Read as the pursuit of a self-enclosed sculptural form, minimalism ostensibly acts in a way which is consistent with the self-critical progression Greenberg describes. Here, though, the very reduction of the sculptural work to a simple geometrical shape threatens to turn this progression against itself. Ironically, in this reading, it is the minimalist presentation of an 'irreducible' form that precipitates the theatrical, forcing attention away from what might be *interior* and so 'proper' and 'necessary' to the work of art.

In response to this threat to the modernist ideal, Fried reconsiders both Greenberg's account of the modernist project and his own earlier view of modernism.[30] It is in this very reformulation of the modernist work, however, that one can trace out contradictions that put into question the very idea of the work of art's legitimation of itself *in its own terms*.

In order to distinguish between the 'literalist' nature of the minimalist object and the modernist projection toward autonomy, Fried now makes a distinction between the formal integrity of the work of art and the physical integrity of the object. Arguing that painting's 'timeless conditions', that is 'the *minimal conditions for something being seen as a painting*', should be seen as distinct from 'what, at a given moment, is capable of compelling conviction, of succeeding as painting', Fried questions Greenberg's account of the modernist projection toward an 'absolute'. Yet, he argues:

This is not to say that painting *has no* essence; it *is* to claim that essence – i.e., that which compels conviction – is largely determined by, and therefore changes continually in response to, the vital work of the recent past. The essence of painting is not something irreducible. Rather, the task of the modernist painter is to discover those conventions that, at a given moment, *alone* are capable of establishing his work's identity as painting.[31]

In other words, the modernist work is not a projection toward that which ultimately legitimates the medium but is a search for *quality* and *value* in the context of a particular set of historical conditions. Yet this particular re-reading, which not only Fried but more recent proponents of modernism and the modernist work have advanced,[32] puts into question the very possibility of the 'essence' and so the 'foundation' which the idea of the work of art's self-legitimation assumes.

If the modernist project within painting is understood to be one which seeks to establish the identity of the medium in a *particular* historical and cultural context, then its teleological aspect, its projection toward the 'viable essence' of all painting, is lost. Yet without such a teleology, the very notion of the modernist work as a work that reveals the interior terms by which an art-form legitimates itself is thrown into question. In these circumstances, the history of modern painting can no longer be regarded as a progression towards that which underlies and legitimates the medium, but must be read as the construction and reconstruction of 'essence'. Yet to describe an 'essence' that is 'constructed', is to enter into a contradiction, for it is to describe an 'essence' penetrated and legitimated by terms beyond its own. Indeed, a work which exemplifies a particular understanding of what painting *can be*, rather than what it has *always been*, can only offer itself as one possibility among others, and in this way declare its own departure from the very idea of an 'essence'. It follows that Fried's yardstick for modernist art, that 'painting of the past whose quality is not in doubt'[33] must also come into question. If there is no constant, no trans-historical *fact* to be revealed from within painting, then the reading of the history of painting becomes a site of dispute over value rather than the discovery of value. If the very qualities that determine the *identity* of painting are themselves subject to historical and, by implication, cultural context, then the criterion for 'success' becomes as much a matter of *who looks* as *what is seen*.

In such circumstances, the modernist project becomes multiple and contingent as its appeal to metanarrative is lost to an awareness of the contingent nature of the legitimacy of the work. The legitimating core of the work of art as Fried describes it here is inseparable from the circumstances, histories and assumptions that have produced its particular aesthetic terms. In fact, here, the modernist work finally loses its meaning, its *possession* of its own definition.

Performance: Allan Kaprow's *Self-Service* (1967) and George Brecht's *Water Yam* (1962)

After these reconsiderations of the object, and in the context of Fried's identification of the 'theatrical' with an 'anti-modernist' corruption of art, one can readily identify a 'postmodern' evasion of stable parameters, meanings and identities with 'performance' emerging from the visual arts in the early 1960s. The 'theatricality' which defines the work of Allan Kaprow and George Brecht, in particular, emerges from a radical reconceiving of the 'object' through an attention to the contingencies the specifically modernist work, in Fried's terms, would transcend or suppress. In the development of these presentations and activities, the very idea of a 'performance' would seem to be bound up with a giving of voice to occurrences that surround, penetrate and disrupt the boundaries of what would be the 'work of art'. Kaprow's 'Happenings for performers only' and Brecht's 'event-scores', in particular, exemplify such strategies, as they invite a questioning of the very realisations they look toward, even at the risk of undermining the final coming into being of a distinct 'thing', of a recognisable and bounded 'work'.

In *Self-Service* of 1967, which, like his earlier 'Happenings', emerges and develops directly out of his work with assemblage and environment, Kaprow pursues an acute fragmentation, dispersing individuals and events in space and time. According to Kaprow's published score, *Self-Service* is to be comprised of a possible 45 events; nine may take place in Boston, ten in New York and 26 in Los Angeles. Each of these events is to be quite isolated in its realisation, the whole pattern of activities emerging across three different states and over a total possible period of four months. Although no one action is directly dependent upon another for its realisation, Kaprow's score allows events to take place simultaneously across the three states. More frequently, activities will simply overlap or remain quite separate. Just as events are separated in place and time so there is little connection between activities through any 'subject', theme or obvious imagery. In his documentation Kaprow notes that in New York, for example:

People stand on empty bridges, on street corners, watch cars pass. After two hundred red ones, they leave.

While at another time:

An empty house. Nails are hammered halfway into all surfaces of rooms, house is locked, hammerers go away.

In Boston:

People tie tar paper around many cars in a supermarket lot.

On another day, twenty or more flash-gun cameras shoot off at the same time all over the supermarket; shopping resumed.

While in Los Angeles:

Cars drive into filling stations, erupt with white foam pouring from windows.

Couples kiss in the midst of the world, go on.[34]

Kaprow's method of working, as well as the strictures surrounding an engagement with the project, serve to further disrupt the physical and conceptual integrity of this set of activities. For the participants there will be no single activity involving the entire group, no set of activities completed by everybody, nor any particular focus serving to define a group experience. Kaprow goes on to specify that the piece is to be 'for performers only', as if to counter any focus that may be defined by the gathering of spectators. Furthermore, while those who would be an audience to *Self-Service* must engage in prescribed activities, Kaprow avoids both rehearsal and repetition. In a conversation with the critic Richard Kostalanetz, published in Kostalanetz's book *The Theatre of Mixed Means* (New York, 1968), Kaprow remarks, 'if you're interested in playing my game, then come and talk it over, and we'll decide who's going to do what at that time. After that, we'll do it.'[35] Once ended, he is quite reluctant to repeat any realisation or to have any person engage in it again. In *Assemblages, Environments and Happenings* he states categorically that, however detailed the preparations or predetermined its rules or strictures, '*Happenings should be performed once only.*'[36]

While Kaprow's rules for performance seemed designed to resist any actual or easily perceivable sense of an organised 'whole', the nature and identity of the individual activities of which the piece is to consist would seem themselves to be rendered unsteady or uncertain in their realisation. In prescribing each activity in the way he does Kaprow usurps their functions, and looks toward a catching of the elements of this 'performance' in a double-bind. Without their usual purposes and sense these largely functional activities might become arbitrary, no longer belonging to the 'everyday' though they are taken directly from it and sometimes remain embedded within it. In the frame of Kaprow's prescription, the identity and value of each action is called into question, just as close attention is called to their enactment or performance. In his essay 'Participation Performance' Kaprow draws attention to the effect of this prescription:

> Intentionally performing everyday life is bound to create some curious kinds of awareness. Life's subject matter is almost too familiar to grasp, and life's formats (if they can be called that) are not familiar enough.[37]

The 'performance' of such activities by those who would be spectators to the 'Happening' also serves to put into question their framing as part of a 'work'. To engage in an activity in a supermarket, for example, is not to discover a single or clear focus but to rehearse a simple action embedded within a flow of 'everyday' events and distractions. Again, Kaprow envisages just such a questioning of the parameters of these elements. In a Happening, he argues:

> the very materials, the environment, the activity of the people in that environment, are the primary images, not the secondary ones. The environment is not a setting for a play ... which is more important than the people ... there is an absolute flow between event and environment.[38]

Displaced from their usual purposes, these activities offer points from which occurrences beyond the artist's control or determination may become a focus of attention. In doing so, the boundaries, even the possibility of drawing parameters around the elements of a 'work', come into question.

Such strategies, however, do not mean that *Self-Service* is simply antithetical to the idea of the 'work of art'. Indeed, the promise these strategies make, their reference to a 'whole', despite the dispersal of elements and focuses, looks toward a negotiation, a testing of identities and meanings, and a catching of events *between* possibilities. Of *Self-Service* Kaprow notes:

> So many things had just that quality of dropping things in the world and then going about your business. The whole thing teetered on the edge of not-quite-art, not-quite-life.[39]

Despite the deliberate confusion of *Self-Service* as a distinct entity, Kaprow's strictures look toward another kind of coherence, one rooted in a shared function or purpose and so in the character of the participant's active engagement. First, then, and through each of the activities the participant engages in, a *self-service* is in some way brought into play. Amongst the 'available activities', Kaprow describes:

> People shout in a subway just before getting off, leaving immediately.
> Many shoppers begin to whistle in aisles of supermarkets. After a few minutes they go back to their shopping.
> In glass booths, people listen to records. They look at each other and dance.
> Some people whistle a tune in the crowded elavator of an office building.
> People enter phone booths, eat sandwiches and drink sodas, look out at the world.[40]

In each of these places of self-service the participant is to make the piece for herself. It is not a single pattern of actions, but a service by oneself to oneself, a common manner of behaviour defined by place, intention and means. At other times the participant is to serve herself in her choice from prescribed activities:

> Everyone watches for either
>   a signal from someone
>   a light to go on in a window
>   a plane to pass directly overhead
>   an insect to land nearby
>   three motorcycles to barrel past.[41]

Kaprow's rules take up and amplify this play of association. In describing the rules of the event to Richard Schechner, Kaprow notes:

all of the events were 'self-service' – a person could choose to participate in as many as he wished down to one; if anything came up – as it will during the summer – a person had the right to cancel out and substitute something else later on.[42]

Although Kaprow specifies the total sum of different events for each state, he does not shape the frequency of these events, their repetition or their timing. At the same time, and while the totality of events remains disjointed and fractured, Kaprow notes that *Self-Service* 'was programmed so that everybody participating knew exactly what else was going on'.[43] In this way, Kaprow's rules promise a balance between a physical involvement with the piece, a direct initiation of activities, and a knowledge of other activities to be initiated elsewhere. As the participant executes her actions so this structure seeks to draw attention between that execution and her knowledge of that in the process of execution or which has or will be executed. In *Assemblages, Environments and Happenings*, Kaprow emphasises that:

Although the participant is unable to do everything and be in all places at once, he knows the overall pattern if not the details. And like the agent in an international spy ring, he knows, too, that what he does devotedly will echo and give character to what others do elsewhere.[44]

Kaprow's strategies would seem designed to draw a participant's attention in two directions at once. What is offered here is the dissolution of what would be a work, as any sense of 'whole', of material or conceptual integrity is broken down, put into question. Paradoxically, though, and at the moment of this dissolution, the viewer-participant's activity is one of building, of a movement toward realisation. Indeed, in taking up the invitations of *Self-Service*, the 'viewer-participant' becomes instrumental not only to the production but also to the reception of the 'Happening' and so to the possibility of its very existence. Kaprow's conception of the participant's experience echoes this point, as he suggests that 'by knowing the scenario and one's particular duties beforehand, a person becomes a real and necessary part of the work. It cannot exist without him.'[45] To play such a game would be to engage once and once only in an activity of building, in the making of a game which is a game of making a 'work of art'. In *Self-Service*, and in these respects, Kaprow's strictures repeatedly provoke a move towards and yet a postponement of a determination of what is or is not a part of that with which the viewer-participant should be concerned. In this sense, *Self-Service* might be best read as the provocation and shaping of moves toward a 'work', and yet, simultaneously, a set of strategies which serve to stave off a closure and so identification of what this work might be. As it is presented by Kaprow, *Self-Service* consists simply of a set of rules that, in their activation by the participant, at once look towards a realisation, and yet seek to stave off any final closure of what would be 'the work', of any end to the process of realisation.

While through his rules Kaprow takes a direct control over the formal operation of *Self-Service* and so aspects of the participant's choices and activities, George Brecht, through his *Water Yam* and other 'event-cards', steps back from even this determining frame. As a result, these 'scores' seem less concerned with the disruption or breaking down of a 'work' than with a catching of attention at a point at which the promise of a work, and the move toward closure, is first encountered.

Through their very slightness, many of the cards presented as part of the *Water Yam*, a boxed edition by Brecht and published first of all by Fluxus in 1962,[46] imply identities of various kinds. *Three Aqueous Events*, a card measuring five by five-and-a-half centimetres, might be taken to be a poem or simple statement. At the same time, it may appear more like a list or a description of a process of change. Then again, it has the qualities of a score, and could be taken as looking towards the performance of three activities in response to 'ice', 'water' and 'steam', or as an invitation to take three events or occurrences as a focus for attention. Considered as a score, the card seems to be even more open and unclear, as it becomes an ambiguous stimulus to something or other that is yet to be made or occur. In doing so, it places its own self-sufficiency into question and explicitly looks towards a decision yet to be made.

In this way, instead of asserting itself as any 'thing' in particular, *Three Aqueous Events* remains pointedly open to suggestion, as if it might embrace any and all of the characteristics a reader, observer or performer may care to assign to it. It may even be that such an 'open-ness' serves to qualify the various responses it invites, provoking an awareness of the contingent nature of any particular determination of the score. Such a level of ambiguity may well disarm the possibility of any single or simple response, perhaps leaving the reader to wonder how one might effectively react to such a lack of definition.

Brecht's own comments only serve to heighten these ambiguities. In an interview with the critic Henry Martin, Brecht argued that through such cards 'I don't demand anything. I'd leave the maximum of freedom

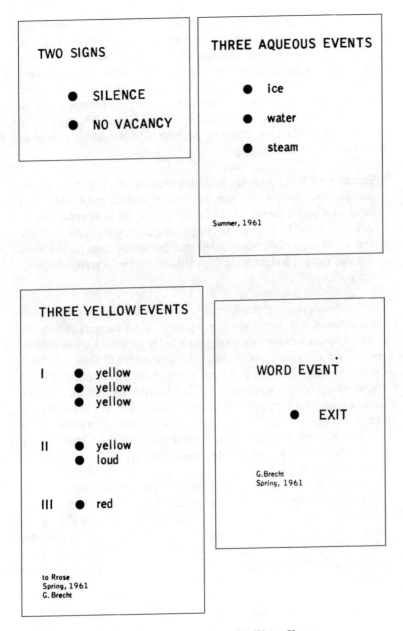

George Brecht, cards from the *Water Yam*,
originally published by Fluxus (New York, 1962)

to everybody.'[47] Yet while dismissing the notion that there might be any particular way to respond, Brecht also suggests that these games are not self-sufficient. He refers to the *Water Yam* cards as 'scores' or 'event-cards'[48] and has stated categorically, and of all his work, be it event-card or object, that 'an event is always intended, or implied'.[49] Henry Martin, who has documented Brecht's work in his book *An Introduction to George Brecht's Book of the Tumbler on Fire* (Milan, 1978), argues that it is necessary to find something to 'do' with what Brecht offers in order to make sense of it:

> Brecht's work is concerned with moments in which mind is active, creative and autonomous. The work resists being appreciated on the basis of a passive perception of what it is; it finds its sense and its function on the basis of some things one can do with it, on the basis, that is, of a possible relationship one can create with it. The work remains opaque and meaningless until one decides actively to collaborate with it.[50]

Such descriptions of the formal nature of this card, however, only seem to make the 'work' towards which it might point further out of reach. A 'collaboration' with the card may involve or look toward an 'event', yet an event is not, particularly, an example of theatre or 'non-theatrical' activity or music or even a private act. According to Brecht, 'event simply has the meaning it has in the dictionary',[51] indicating perhaps 'a thing that happens' and as such could imply any or all of these things. It would seem that in seeking to collaborate actively with that which Brecht offers, the reader or viewer must define not only the particular terms of any card but the formal identity or identities of the 'event' it may provoke.

Brecht's realisations of *Three Aqueous Events* reflect such a process. Henry Martin notes that Brecht has made a film in which he performed the piece,[52] while Michael Kirby in his anthology *Happenings* (New York, 1965) describes a theatre performance of *Three Aqueous Events* in which Brecht poured water into three glasses.[53] Brecht himself has recalled using the event-card as the basis for another object, score and event:

> A canvas with the word 'Glace' in the upper left corner and the word 'Buee' on the bottom at the right and a glass in the middle half filled with water. It's a score, it's a realisation, and what's more it's an event as the water is evaporating.[54]

In contrast to Brecht, Allan Kaprow was prompted to make himself a drink in response to the flexibility of the score. In his article on 'Non-theatrical Performance' he notes that he 'once made a delicious iced tea on the stimulation of the piece and thought about it while drinking'.[55] Henry Martin goes on to suggest that a realisation of *Three Aqueous Events* could take almost any form, all of which would be equally appropriate:

A work such as this ... is in constant existence no matter what the modality of forms of human consciousness directed to it. Simply reading the work is a performance of the work, and the same can be said of simply thinking it, and one can think of it as three words, or three sounds, or three physical entities. It can be oral, aural, tactile, visual, taste or any other kind of experience; it can be of any duration and of any order of dimension.[56]

In presenting a score which is so ambiguous, Brecht at once stimulates a move towards closure and intervenes to stave off its possibility. Clearly, in this reading no individual choice can provide a final resolution to *Three Aqueous Events*, despite the fact that it offers itself as a 'work' yet to be realised. Whatever the reader 'does' or chooses, the possibility of another choice threatens to displace the move toward 'realisation' at the moment in which it is made. In his article, 'George Brecht: An Art of Multiple Implications', the critic Jan Van der Marck sets this aspect of Brecht's work against Marcel Duchamp's earlier consideration of the observer. Here, he argues:

Duchamp's notion that it is the observer who completes the work of art becomes in Brecht's interpretation the notion of the observer forever trying, like Sisyphus, but never able to finish the work – or dispose of the idea.[57]

Such invitations to the reader or viewer to discover her own implication in the meaning and identity of things permeate Brecht's work. Among many kinds of objects, Brecht exhibits signs which exemplify the status he wishes to lend to the various aspects of his work. He notes:

To me, all the various parts of my work amount to the same thing. I think of my works as events, and the signs exist to create the possibility of an event. When you go into a room and find a sign that says 'No

Smoking' you have to make a decision. And to make a decision is an
event.[58]

Such an object cannot be separated from the event of its being read.
Although different in their mechanism from *Three Aqueous Events*, the
signs remain parallel to it. To discover the 'object' is to have made a
relationship, to have made, in Brecht's terms, an 'arrangement'. Furthermore, just as the 'object' has no independent identity so, by implication,
the viewer can never be neutral, can never attend to a thing that somehow remains apart from her. In pursuing this notion of an arrangement
Brecht attempts to shift the focus of his work entirely from the 'object'
as a thing in which properties reside and to a shifting set of relationships
operating through stimulus and response. In this way, Brecht's activities
proceed on the notion that to perceive is to constitute and so be respons-
ible for that which is perceived. In conversation with Henry Martin, he
concludes:

> for me, an object does not exist outside of people's contact with it.
> There is no 'real' object as opposed to out idea of the object. The only
> object that exists is the object there and me here. You with the object
> at a different moment is a different object.[59]

Here there can be no separation of the 'work' from the viewer, nor
can 'art' be considered a special case, something self-contained and
self-justifying, but is itself an effect of an 'arrangement', a point defined
by and subject to shifting processes of negotiation. Art and the work of
art are not 'things' but occurrences, which the artist's making can no
more be said to give an identity to than the viewer's act of seeing. Consistently with this, Brecht's focus falls not so much upon the 'work of
art' as upon the relationships within which this very notion of 'a work'
is bound. In an early interview of 1965 with the artists Marcel Alocco
and Ben Vautier, he suggested that 'Everyone's a creator ... I never think
of what I do as art or not art. It's an activity, that's all.'[60]
In declaring their incompletion and attempting to stave off closure,
Brecht's 'scores' endanger the idea that they may present, make or look
towards a 'work' in any tangible sense. Yet this very evasion of a final
realisation is pursued in an address to a process of 'arrangement' on
which the 'work of art' is contingent. It follows that these 'scores' are
not an attempt to provoke a particular end, but to make visible that
which the work depends upon but which it cannot contain, to trip up and
make apparent the move towards the 'event' of its definition. Such

activities exemplify a reaching towards instabilities and contingencies which evade the'self-legitimating' work of art, and engage instead with events, transactions and negotiations which might look, literally, towards a 'borderline art'. For Brecht, it seems such fragile contents are entirely at the centre of his concerns:

Sounds barely heard; sights barely distinguished – borderline art. See which way it goes (it should be possible to miss it).[61]

Chapter 3

Looking Beyond Form:
Foreman, Kirby, Wilson

While the debates surrounding the minimalist object provide positions from which a 'postmodern' corruption of the boundaries of the work can be set against various steps from the object and into theatre, the forms and methods of minimal and serial sculpture also offer points from which developments in theatre practice can be read against the postmodern.

In the work of Richard Foreman, Robert Wilson and Michael Kirby, a concern for structural and formal pattern is evident in presentations offered in the more conventional surroundings of a theatre. Read in relation to familiar models of representational drama, such performance can be seen as a retreat from 'content' in the name of a 'New Formalism',[1] an increasingly self-absorbed focus upon form and structure in its own right. Set against minimal art, however, this refutation of 'content' seems not so much a sign of a faith in the self-supporting nature of form as an attempt to throw the viewer's effort to read the performance sharply back upon itself. Such strategies put into question not only the very possibility of an 'autonomous' form, but take their place in a more elaborate questioning of the very means through which these performances constitute themselves and the readings they seem, variously, to invite.

At the most immediate level, connections between the work of Kirby, Wilson and Foreman, and the practices and vocabulary of minimal art are apparent. Michael Kirby's later work in theatre and performance is clearly shaped by his work as a visual artist. Following an engagement with 'Happenings' in the early 1960s and a realisation, through contact with the composer John Cage's use of chance method, of the validity of 'a giving up of the aesthetic decision',[2] Kirby was involved as a visual artist with minimal and serial painting and sculpture. In his work with the Structuralist Workshop, founded in 1975 with his production of *Eight People*, Kirby brought these 'systematic' methods of composition to bear directly on to performance. Subsequently, in pieces such as *First Signs of Decadence* (1985), Kirby applied strict and often complex rules to the generation of plays in an otherwise 'realistic' style in order to overcome aspects of his own intention while foregrounding form and structure. For Richard Foreman both the practices of systematic art and the implications of the minimalist object provided a clarification of work rooted in a variety of sources. Under the influence of film-makers such as Jonas Mekas and Jack Smith, notions of performance developed by Yvonne Rainer[3] and the work of various 'poets and non-theatrical people',[4] Foreman's early work systematically inverted the 'good practice' he had acquired through his training as a playwright. In this context, Foreman suggests, at the time of his first *Ontological-Hysteric Theatre* production, *Angelface* of 1968:

> minimalism and a very superficial encounter with some of the ideas of Alchemy ... were really at the centre of the way I began ... how the stuff was mixed and remixed or boiled and reboiled. And the repetition of that activity, again and again and again.[5]

Unlike Kirby and Foreman, Robert Wilson's work has important roots in entirely non-artistic sources. While he studied painting in Paris in 1962 and then trained as an architect in New York, Wilson's experience of being cured of a speech impediment in his late teens by a dancer, Mrs Bird Hoffman, proved as formative as his involvement with the visual arts. During his college studies he worked with children, teaching theatre and working on performance projects designed by his students.[6] After 1965 Wilson came to work with brain-damaged and handicapped children, applying 'movement exercises to release tension'[7] which often involved extreme slow-motion and were drawn directly from his memory of Bird Hoffman's work.

In developing his early operas, and while pursuing a distinctly architectural concern for space, Wilson drew directly on the experiences, behaviour and writing of the children with whom he worked. *The King of Spain* (1969), *The Life and Times of Sigmund Freud* (1969) and, particularly, *Deafman Glance* (1970) called on Wilson's work with Raymond Andrews, a deaf and mute teenager he had met in 1968. From 1973 Wilson collaborated with Christopher Knowles who, although

born with severe brain damage, played a prominent part in the develop-
ment and performances of *The Life and Times of Joseph Stalin* (1973),
A Letter for Queen Victoria (1974), *The $ Value of Man* (1975) and
Einstein on the Beach (1976).

At the same time, Wilson's first presentations in New York, around
1967 and 1968, came to be strongly related to a prevailing minimalist
aesthetic as his concern 'to go back to the simplest thing I could do ...
how do I walk ... how do I sit in the chair and walk off'[8] emerged in performance. To some of his collaborators the influence of minimal art and
music seemed evident, even where Wilson's later and often visually
extravagant presentations appeared to move in quite another direction.
Franny Brooks, who participated in Wilson's earliest work, notes that:

> Those early pieces were very sparse – I think he was influenced a lot
> by John Cage around this time ... the concert he played with one note
> ... he was very influenced by this minimalist thinking. I don't know
> what happened when he went into *King of Spain*, but somehow he
> became much more baroque, a sort of combination of baroque and the
> minimal.[9]

For Kirby and Foreman, in particular, and in a recognition of the 'theatricality' of the minimalist object, 'minimalism' is associated not with
self-sufficiency and an exclusion of the viewer, but a recognition of
relation and contingency. Foreman observes that 'structure is always a
combination of the THING and the PERCEIVING of it',[10] while Kirby, similarly, does not understand either the work or its structures to exist in
any way independently of a process of negotiation with the viewer.
Stressing the paramount importance of the address to the nature and
effect of structure to his Structuralist Theatre, Kirby qualifies this
emphasis, writing that:

> 'Structure' is being used to refer to the way the parts of a work relate
> to each other, how they 'fit together' in the mind to form a particular
> configuration. This fitting together does not happen 'out there' in the
> objective work; it happens in the mind of the spectator.[11]

Rather than move towards an exclusion of the viewer from the terms
by which the work is defined, in this work 'structure' is foregrounded in
order to address the viewer's act of reading. Indeed, Foreman understands the self-referentiality of the minimalist object in precisely this
way. By excluding any relationship between its parts, he assumes, this

sculpture does not turn inward, but reflects back outward, forcing the viewer's attention away from what might be 'interior' to the work and back on to the act of reading. In referring directly to minimal and systematic work in his *Ontological-Hysteric Manifesto I* (1972) he notes:

> as Stella, Judd, *et al.* realised several years ago ... one must reject composition in favour of shape (or something else) ... Why? Because the resonance must be between the head and the object. The resonance between the elements of the object is now a DEAD THING.[12]

Richard Foreman: *Pandering to the Masses: A Misrepresentation* (1975)

In *Pandering to the Masses: A Misrepresentation*,[13] Richard Foreman offers a stream of elements that repeatedly refer to one or more plays or narratives but which remain a flow of fragments, incompletions, new beginnings and shifts in logic. Employing references to character, narrative, symbol and discourse, the performance rapidly and overtly collages conflicting elements and categories one upon the other in such a way as to defeat any sense of unity. Not only the structure, but the design, set construction, performance style, as well as the self-reflexive nature of the moment-to-moment progression of the piece, all serve to put the conventional function of its elements into question.

Shortly after its beginning, the performance is announced to be only the prologue to *Pandering to the Masses: A Misrepresentation*, at the centre of which will be a play within a play, *Fear*. Yet *Fear* offers only the reported entry of the personification of fear, whose invisibility provides a cue for the 'characters' of *Pandering to the Masses* to discuss their lack of fear. Shortly afterwards, Foreman's own taped voice announces a 'return to the central narrative of the play entitled *Pandering to the Masses: A Misrepresentation*'.[14] Like the title itself, which pointedly leaves open the question of precisely where the misrepresentation lies, the performance pursues uncertainties, repeatedly shifting its ground in order to put itself into question.

As the lights come up the audience faces a space only 16 feet wide and some 20 feet deep. 'Max' sits centre, looking directly at the spectators. A man sits at a bicycle down-centre; he pedals rapidly but the bicycle does not move. Foreman's taped voice announces that the play concerns Rhoda's introduction to a secret society concerned with a very particular kind of knowledge. The performer playing Max exclaims: 'You ...

understand ... NOTHING!' Foreman's voice informs the audience that they
will not understand. A buzzer. The voice announces a recapitulation. Yet
the recapitulation signals a new action; Rhoda enters, downstage, discovering a letter. The voice reflects, in a contradictory manner, on the
audience's mode of thought, supposing that they think through 'the
associative method ... Each thought is accompanied by overtones which
are images but may not be pictures but are, certainly.'[15] This in turn cues
what might be a play on such association:

> A buzzer. Music overlaps. RHODA, SOPHIA and ELEANOR revealed
> naked at the top of a hill. Three men run down the hill with giant
> pencils and wave them threateningly at MAX. Then the women start
> down the hill, and when the music stops, turn sideways in provoc-
> ative poses.[16]

The walls at the rear have opened to reveal a 30-foot raked stage. Max
looks at the women through the wrong end of the telescope. A buzzer.
Music. Max dances as a wall slides in, blocking his view of the women
as the voice considers what would be the nature of Max's motivation for
dancing in the conventional theatre. Max stops dancing. The prologue is
announced, the play itself 'will begin in, perhaps, five minutes'. Then:

> MAX: (Holding out his hand) Now I want some water.
> VOICE: Now, he reaches out his hand. What could go into his hand.
> MAX: Another hand.
> > (RHODA enters, puts her hand in his.)[17]

The dialogue, like the commentaries and actions, prove unpredictable
and open to more than one logic. Max and Rhoda talk to each other, but
might both be the voice's own reflections, and yet Max shares in this
control and is, in any case, physically at the centre. Rather than manifest
any single familiar or conventional logic the play self-consciously
reflects on the processes which underlie its own construction and reception. Yet even this does not provide concrete ground, as the demonstration of any particular process seems to disappear under the weight of
repeated interruptions, ironic digressions, slapstick exchanges or simple
contradictions and changes of sense. Instead of attending to each other
through the play, the performers present themselves directly to the audience, who are brightly lit. Speaking unemotionally and with a variety of
inflections,[18] the performers drain their behaviour of the emotional

contents to which scenes and dialogue refer, throwing suggestions of character and fictional interaction starkly into relief.

Just as the organisation of the sequence of elements and the distribution of elements in space serves to frustrate the building of a unified picture, so the presentation of the theatre-space reveals Foreman's choices. Props and furniture are placed in order to show and emphasise the basic design of the space. Strings which run across its width, rather like lines in a diagram, demonstrate its division and are manipulated by the performers to accentuate and create frames and focuses. The peculiar nature of Foreman's Ontological-Hysteric theatre also allows a continual remaking of the performance space involving, in *Pandering to the Masses*, a transformation of depth from 12 to as much as 75 feet.

As if such means were not enough to ensure the audience's self-conscious remove from the sequence of actions and images, *Pandering to the Masses* employs a system which serves to fragment the dialogue in the most arbitrary of ways. The exchanges of the four principal performers are taped, 'each separate word being spoken by a different one of those four performers in sequence, no matter who was listed in the script'.[19] In turn, the voice of each performer is isolated on one of four speakers, placed one at each of the four corners of the audience. As the dialogue proceeds, each performer speaks key words over the taped dialogue, while certain lines remain unrecorded, to be spoken live for emphasis. Foreman's own voice is heard in deep, measured tones from the furthest rear speaker, as if to counterbalance the focus offered by the physical presence of the performers.

Like each of his Ontological-Hysteric productions, *Pandering to the Masses* is shaped through Foreman's concern to attend to his act of writing at each successive moment in which he writes. His scripts evidence, first of all, a continually renewed attention to the present moment, and are a product of an attempt to resist a projection toward continuity and unity through the material he commits to the page. In practice, Foreman's process involves a literal and continual 'beginning again' through which he arrives at a structure of repeated 'false starts'.[20] Key to his method, he suggests, is:

> Sleep. I take naps during the day. To 'clear' my mind, so that I can 'begin again' – start a new day, as it were, whose writing comes from a new place ... I 'fire' bursts of writing ... then, to avoid being dragged into the river of that 'discourse which has just gotten under way,' I need to move back to the firing area. I SLEEP, I NEGATE THE DRIFT of the writing burst I've just fired, its tendency to live its own

life and write its own development. I wake up cleansed, and fire
again![21]

Such processes result in work which is not only acutely self-referen-
tial but in certain respects paradoxical. In particular, Foreman's method
involves a continual attempt to observe and defeat his writing's coming
into being as a 'play' and so to escape the formal and thematic implications of whatever elements he introduces. In his *Ontological Hysteric
Manifesto I* (1972) Foreman emphasises that one must 'write by thinking *against* the material ... don't sustain anything'.[22] Yet at the same time
the very elements that occur to Foreman, or which he chooses, invite
precisely the kind of attention he apparently wishes to deny himself and
his audience. Just as *Pandering to the Masses* begins with the promise
of an explanation which, we are told, will not be realised, so signs of
plot or narrative are evident, yet no plot emerges. In his staging, too,
Foreman extends precisely this same mode of self-consciousness, looking back towards the fragmentation of his writing rather than forward
towards any kind of final coherence. He notes:

> the staging ... is not an attempt to CONVINCE the audience of the play's
> reality or verisimilitude ... but rather an effort to rewrite the text back
> into manuscript ... It is a CONTINUATION of my writing process.[23]

While indications of individual roles are clear, the dispersal and fragmentation of dialogue, the performers' attention to the audience rather
than each other, as well as the self-reflexive nature of the text, work
against a coherent reading of these indications and frustrate the coming into being of any particular 'characterisation'. Instead Foreman
continually returns to the various promises such elements may make in
the belief that 'the gesture, the impulse which comes to nothing (which
doesn't fulfil itself) ... fulfils that other thing which is truthfully operating through me'.[24] In other words, the 'false start' returns him (and, by
implication, the viewer) to an awakening to his own act of construction,
either at the point of writing, directing or reading.

Such attacks on sense and continuity, which typify Foreman's
Ontological-Hysteric productions, clearly go further than a disruption of
the conventional unities of a play or representational piece of theatre. At
each successive moment Foreman would seem to direct his strategies
towards a wrong-footing of the viewer's move towards closure, towards
interpretation and understanding. Such a resistance to a reading of the elements of what would be the 'play' through the construction of a sensible

or organised pattern, serves to stave off the emergence of the 'object', a sense of 'whole' to which meaning and purpose might be attributed. For Foreman, it seems, the emergence of this 'object' is synonymous with the viewer's escape from responsibility. In his *Ontological Hysteric: Manifesto II* (1974) he remarks that 'if each moment is new, if we die to each moment as it arises, we are alive. Development (sequential) is death. Is objectification.'[25]

Such objectification, Foreman argues, is brought into play by habit, by a desire for security and, ultimately, perceptual and intellectual sleep. He concludes that 'we are taught to see objects (rather than perceptual acts) and we are by those objects, enslaved'.[26] It follows that rather than celebrating and reinforcing this inheritance art might 'begin the process of freeing men by calling into doubt the solidity of objects – and laying bare the fact that it is a web of relations that exists, only ... '[27]

Yet although the systematic fragmentation of Foreman's productions and his self-conscious address to the process of looking involve a rejection of the illusion of the 'object', this work pointedly retains its trappings. In contrast to the work of John Cage, in particular, but also a wide range of departures in art, performance and dance that have employed chance method in composition and performance,[28] Foreman pursues what he sees as a route that evades both conventional representational schemes and aleatory processes. Foreman associates the attempt to 'give up' meaning through chance operations with another kind of 'objectification' and understands his own approach not as an escape from such 'distortions' but an awakening to them. In his first manifesto he lists three principal distortions:

1) logic – as in realism, which we reject because the mind already 'knows' the next move and so is not alive to that next move.
2) chance & accident & the arbitrary – which we reject because in too short a time each choice so determined becomes equally predictable as 'item produced by chance, accident, etc.'
3) the new possibility (what distorts with its weight) – a subtle insertion between logic and accident, which keeps the mind alive as it evades over quick integration into the mental system. CHOOSE THIS ALWAYS![29]

Consistently with this, *Pandering to the Masses* continually returns to indications of representation and signification in order to wrong-foot the expectations such indications may bring into play. Instead of inviting a reading of the 'object' or attempting to escape its terms altogether,

Pandering to the Masses repeatedly renews a promise of the object's coming into being yet always seeks to frustrate the continuities and coherences on which it depends. Thus the performance undercuts itself as it traces out, at each successive moment, expectations that are systematically let down. This leads, Foreman suggests, to a critique that 'is the body and flesh of the play', and that, because it is the very substance of the performance, becomes, paradoxically, 'the critique of a play that isn't there'.[30] It is a 'play' whose elements seem continually to come into view but which never finally appears, a play whose realisation and so closure is perpetually staved off.

It follows that while Foreman is concerned to disrupt the 'object', it is the process of disruption, rather than the presence or otherwise of the object itself, that is his primary concern. In this way, the object, or at least its possibility, remains in play at the moment at which it is dissolved. Foreman emphasises:

> I do think that some sort of *dissolving* of the object – which is invariably dishonest in its need to convince, is desirable. But what seems most interesting to me is to dissolve the art-work as self-consciously as possible ... I'd like to build it into the object ... in such a way that my actual making of the work is a *being-there* with the dissolving process.[31]

Such a tension is fundamental not only to the notion of the 'object' in Foreman's work, but also to his treatment of particular elements. Operating through what can be read as a systematic distraction from possible points of view or continuities, Foreman frequently disrupts any sense of centre by the presentation of simultaneous and unreconcilable focuses. Rather than simply present contradictory events, he offers a collage of competing points of attention bound to one another through a single structure or pattern. Thus Foreman will add whistles to the dominant beat of music.[32] He will frequently frame, punctuate or counterpoint dialogue with 'foghorns, thuds, pings, boings, glass shatterings, drum rolls, bells, whistles and screams',[33] disrupting the rhythm and meaning of the exchange. The actor's manipulation of the strings running across the space may at once reveal Foreman's design of a scene and bring 'material that has less than official status within the scene'[34] to the attention of the audience by framing parts of the body or objects. In this way, while many of the elements Foreman introduces play on the spectator's expectations, and even imply some future continuity, each element is placed in such a way as to disarm another, as different expectations are played against each other. Here, Foreman suggests, 'the field of the play is distorted by the objects within the play, so that each object distorts each other object and the mental pre-set is excluded'.[35] Similarly, the performance style Foreman has fostered can be understood as another means of disarming that which would, at face value, seem to be offered in the text. Working within a precise scenographic design into which performers are placed without regard to psychological continuities, Foreman chose in his early work to use non-actors; performers free of a vocabulary through which they might attempt to draw a continuity from the text. Such a lack of technique allows a draining of psychological depth and the disarming of what might be, by implication, an emotional content.

In her work with Foreman since 1971, Kate Manheim, who remained Foreman's principal performer until the late 1980s, sought to extend these qualities into a more specific vocabulary. Her physical work, Manheim notes, is marked by a breaking up of the continuities of movement and an effort to always work 'against what comes naturally to the body'.[36] Similarly, she focuses upon her own presence as a performer rather than any notion of role or developing mood, alternating in performance between attending to her own sense of presence, which the physical difficulty she pursues serves to heighten, and allowing her mind to dissociate from the text and wander.[37] Through such techniques, she suggests, 'I try to keep myself off-balance ... to keep myself in a state when I'm always surprised by what I'm doing or what's happening.'[38] Thus while the play offers signs of character, Manheim does not pursue any coherent characterisation, and while Manheim looks out towards the audience, considering her own presence, the text provides no direct voice with which she can articulate this focus.

In this way, Foreman's work can be understood as an attempt to place elements in such a manner as to provoke reverberations between the expectations or possibilities each brings into play and a context which diffuses or distracts from the realisation of any particular set of expectations. This is not simply a matter of the disruption of a projection forwards, but rather involves indications of character, emotion, plot and significance being confounded at the moment of their appearance by their framing and manner of presentation. Such a pattern does not look directly toward a plurality of 'interpretations', but towards a 'suspension' of interpretation, toward the moment before a decision is made, in order that the fact of the decision rather than its consequences might be revealed. In his first manifesto Foreman argues:

Only one theatrical problem exists now: How to create a stage performance in which the spectator experiences the danger of art not as
involvement or risk or excitement ... but rather the danger as a
possible *decision* he (spectator) may make upon the occasion of con-
fronting the work of art.[39]

In these respects, Foreman's work points towards the contingent
nature of its own means and seeks to expose this contingency by tripping
up and revealing the audience's bringing of the 'object' into play. In
doing so, the work looks toward the provocation of a self-reflexive
attention in the audience analogous to that self-awareness Foreman pursues in his generation of the text:

The result of being awake (seeing): You are in two places at once (and
ecstatic). Duo-consciousness: 1. You see 2. You see yourself seeing.[40]

It follows from this that form, here, is not to be understood as something within which meaning or significance inheres, but is literally performative, a strategy or set of moves which serve to reveal the fact of its
own conventional nature. In this work, where 'the subject is not anything that you can see',[41] form and subject are understood to be arbitrary
and conventional in their significance, serving as means to address the
negotiation towards meaning rather than anything they can concretely
embody. Hence:

form isn't a container (of content) but rather a rule for generating a
possible 'next move.' That's where the subject is (in that next move,
dictated or made possible by the form). The commonly-thought-of
content or subject is the pretext to set a process in operation, and that .
process is the real subject.[42]

Michael Kirby: *First Signs of Decadence* (1985)

In contrast to Foreman's Ontological-Hysteric Theatre Michael Kirby's
plays and productions with the Structuralist Workshop have been characterised by the incorporation of conventional forms and styles. *First Signs
of Decadence* (1985), which Kirby describes as a 'drawing room play',[43]
is set in a wealthy apartment in Berlin in 1931, where five characters
meet to present the first reading of a new play to potential backers. As the
piece unfolds the audience is introduced to Beatrice Walden, the author

of a new play, Dr Gottfried Schernchen, the author of a popular book of psychology, Señora Rosella San Cristofa, the wife of a wealthy industrialist, and Elfriede Elpner and John Charles Fort, both actors. Typically, the reference to genre is immediately apparent and so a stable context through which the play may be read implicit. Consistently with this, and as always, Kirby writes toward a realistic performance style, arguing that 'theatre to me is realistic' and 'we all understand realism'.[44]

A concern for structure, however, operates through this play without regard for the conventional unities and transparencies of realistic drama. Rather than directly support the realism itself, the structure of *First Signs of Decadence* is determined by a complex array of rules to which the interaction of characters as well as entrances, exits, lighting, music, and even patterns of emotional response, are subject. In the first act, as the characters meet in anticipation of the reading, actors may stand or sit in only nine places, each of which 'is related to the classical stage directions of "up" and "down," of "left," "centre" and "right" found in those books on directing'.[45] Only three of the five actors may be on stage at any one time, one performer leaving as another enters. Every 25 seconds all three actors move to new positions. In this context 'every combination of three, out of the nine, positions is used once; none is used more than once'.[46] By the end of the act, each actor will have been on stage for the same amount of time. In the short second act the characters address the audience as if they were the backers awaiting the reading, while their dialogue is structured around repeated words and phrases. Once each character has addressed the audience directly the act ends. Finally, in the third act, the characters move between eight positions closely related but not identical to those of the first and may only speak while moving. Made up of 31 units, each character is alone for 30 seconds, appears once with every other character for one minute, while every combination of three and four characters appears, respectively, for 90 seconds and two minutes. Finally, all five characters appear simultaneously for two-and-a-half minutes. As the act progresses, various characters are seen in recurring stage-pictures. These rules, Kirby suggests, 'give their activity an entirely different perceptual quality than that of the first act, even if the spectator does not consciously understand the patterning'.[47]

In setting a realistic style against such arbitrary patterns, Kirby sets up conflicts and tensions that cannot readily be resolved by the actor or the audience. Kirby himself stresses the importance of this difficulty, seeing a 'tension between the representational and non-representational aspects' through which the performance is always being 'torn apart'[48] as fundamental to the piece. For the actor in *First Signs of Decadence* this tension is evident in the necessity to justify behaviour which may seem unjustifiable, as actions generated by a formal logic fall into an ostensibly realistic scheme. For the audience, the interdependence of these two schemes serves to bring apparently irreconcilable readings into the same space. Kirby himself suggests that this tension is a key to the piece, observing that 'the structuring works against the traditional dramatic material ... involving and juxtaposing two modes of thought'.[49]

Such juxtaposition does not constitute an attack on realism or formalism as such. Indeed, the structures of *First Signs of Decadence* are not simply set against a realism but invite the audience to read a realism through, and despite, an obvious formal patterning. The structures themselves are manifested through a self-conscious display of the conventions realism has fostered but which are normally rendered transparent. Here, then, the 'rules' of realism are effectively deployed against themselves as the piece attempts not so much to defeat realism as to qualify its reception, working at once 'with and against common expectations and conventions'.[50] In this way the performance can be seen as declaring the conventional nature of realism despite its efficacy, inviting an engagement which may observe at once the nature and effect of the 'realistic' style. Kirby emphasises that 'realistic acting has nothing to do, for me, with suspension of disbelief', arguing that:

> it's a marvellous thing in the theatre if an actor acts realistically and you don't say, 'Wow, how realistic!' You say, 'Wow, what an actor!' I want the second one ... we realise it's acting and yet it's so real.[51]

Just as *First Signs of Decadence* resists an unselfconscious reading of style and structure, so its apparent subject-matter reflects on these tensions and disrupts any straightforward reading of meaning. Here the characters' own discussions may frequently be read both as dialogue in a realistic drama and as self-reflexive commentaries on the formal nature and significance of *First Signs of Decadence*. Caught between opposing possibilities, meaning becomes subject to dispute despite the clarity of the play's elements.

Ostensibly concerned with the reading of Beatrice Walden's new play to potential backers, the nature and significance of the dramatic presentation around which *First Signs of Decadence* is shaped remains elusive. While the characters prepare themselves for the reading in act one and preface the reading to the audience in act two, neither the play nor its title or subject-matter are ever presented. Act three offers only the aftermath of the reading, while the response of the backers and the future of the play are left a matter for speculation. Instead we discover simply that the play may lack a centre. In response, Elfriede, an actress, offers to play the male role of Moreau, so following the advice of Dr Schernchen's popular book, *Dreams, Symbols and the Rational Mind,* which takes the androgenous figure of Mephistopheles as 'a perfect balance of sexual dynamics. A centre from which all experiences radiate.'[52] Read through her possible motivations, Elfriede's suggestion is clearly self-serving. In the formal context of the piece as a whole, though, it is ironic, as her suggestion implies that Beatrice's play, and so *First Signs of Decadence*, might best be centred around an ambiguity. As if to compound this the ambiguity has been drawn from Dr Schernchen who intermittently presents himself as interpreter and interpolater of the new play.

Here, too, another aspect of *First Signs of Decadence* is brought into play through the reference to an ambiguous sexuality. While Dr Schernchen implies that John Charles is homosexual and, in doing so, associates homosexuality with a moral degeneration, he too comes to be implicated in a decadence. *Dreams, Symbols and the Rational Mind,* it seems, might not only be the product of a corrupt scientism but may also serve to legitimate Nazi persecution. More generally, as evidence of anti-Jewish violence in the streets sporadically filters through to the apartment, the characters' own attitudes to the rise of Nazi power remain ambivalent. It appears, too, that government figures, presumably Nazis, may be present in the audience and at various times there is excitement at the possibility that the state itself might support their production.

Beatrice's play, too, it seems, may exemplify another decadence. Rosella associates the play with late nineteenth-century aestheticism, observing that it is 'quite symbolist ... a neo-symbolist play'.[53] Later, Beatrice is accused in her absence of producing a pornography which feeds off a moral and aesthetic decadence. It is a pornography for 'collectors, aesthetes' produced by 'people with taste'.[54] The evidence of this work, however, seems far from pornographic, consisting merely of photographs promoting the benefits of nudism. In turn, Beatrice addresses her potential backers in a way that suggests either a desire for her art to be free of social and moral responsibility or that her audience should decry art without moral direction. She declares:

> We believe that theatre is an art that should be produced by people with taste. We're looking for those who would like to counteract the systematic degradation of art in our society today.[55]

Such ambiguities are reproduced by *First Signs of Decadence* at a formal level too. Indeed, the application of formal patterns 'conceived sep-
arately from the subject matter' and 'completely unrelated to characters
and events'[56] to material referring to the rise of the Nazis, the persecution of the Jews and the moral responsibilities of art might be understood
as a pre-eminent example of aesthetic and moral decadence. Here *First
Signs of Decadence* is itself implicated in the various notions of moral
and aesthetic degeneration it brings into play. At the same time, such a
conflict may also serve to put the possibility of an actual decadence into
question, as the play's self-reflexive and shifting commentaries on its
own formal nature takes this issue into its possible subject-matter.
Finally, while the meaning of decadence remains ambiguous, the attitude of the play itself becomes deeply ambivalent. Here, it seems, if the
play itself can be accused of being decadent, this is because of its calculated demonstration of the very slipperiness of the meaning of decadence, and so the fact that this 'slipperiness' has become not simply a
'theme' but the key to its formal construction. Kirby himself argues that
the play will tend to disrupt the attempt to read its 'meanings', particularly if one seeks to discover coherent readings rooted in theme or
content. He remarks:

> I don't want to do something that has one answer ... I would like to do
> something that's completely open to many contradictory experiences
> all of which are equally 'correct' ... the way to try and do it is to build
> in contradictions and not to tack everything down, building openings
> where it can escape.[57]

As if to draw attention to this dilemma, the characters themselves
periodically consider the meanings of their own actions and the events
they find themselves caught up in. In doing so, however, each of them
seems only to put particular meanings further out of reach. In act one,
following a moment of silence, Elfriede asks after Schernchen's consideration of the symbolic nature of silence in his book. Schernchen, however, seems able only to consider the formal function and character of a
symbol rather than its meaning, noting that 'I'm sure if we thought
about it, we'd find it symbolic.'[58] Later, he announces that when he
speaks to the potential backers he will point out the archetypes within
the play in order to 'help comprehension'.[59] Faced with the audience in
act two, though, this evades him and he stands silently, re-enacting the
silence he suggested we might find symbolic. Finally he reveals the
silence to be merely a ploy, declaring 'I thought that would be a good

way of getting everyone's attention.' Yet the repetition is immediately followed by a slip of the tongue by John Charles, who is then given to expand, unself-consciously, on Schernchen's earlier conclusion:

SCHERNCHEN: Was it symbolic?
JOHN CHARLES: I'm sure if we thought about it we'd find it symbolic. (TO AUDIENCE) That kind of thing is only serious if it recurs.[60]

As the piece progresses such formal repetitions and symmetries repeatedly pose the question of where the meaning lies, while confusing what seemed to be the particular meanings of actions, costume, objects and photographs. In turn, what would appear, at one moment or another, to be safe assumptions about the five roles are quickly thrown into question as clues to attitudes and relationships are read differently at different times by different characters. During this process, individual characters even comment on the way in which such repetition itself invites consideration of the nature and meaning of events, so pushing the play towards a more and more open reflexivity. Faced with yet another coincidence, Beatrice comments on the compelling nature of the patterns which, while sublimated by realistic circumstance and relationship, are nevertheless making their presence felt:

Earlier someone made a mistake about the address. Now, someone is lost. Neither by itself would be unusual. Together, they are very unusual. Together they make one question the very order and balance and symmetry of everyday occurrences.[61]

Rather than support the articulation or invite the reading of coherent themes or points of view, form and structure in this 'Structuralist' play serve to provoke an awareness of the contingency of meaning. Such work might be considered formalist, yet these formal strategies are, in themselves, no more the 'subject-matter' or centre of the work than the realistic elements they organise and frame. Here form is not an end in itself, nor is it allowed to remain transparent. Like Foreman's Ontological-Hysteric theatre, the concerns of this mode of performance is not embodied within a form or content but are to be found at the moment at which one acts upon the other and meanings are destabilised. In *First Signs of Decadence* the possibility of meaning is always present but particular meanings are subject to shifting, ambiguous and self-reflexive relationships and points of view. Here, the viewer is presented with a

form and style of work which, through its very familiarity, invites readings which are then displaced and confounded, a set of moves which
repeatedly demonstrate the instability of any particular meaning and so
which stave off and frustrate the move toward a final closure.

Robert Wilson: *Deafman Glance* (1970)

Robert Wilson's *Deafman Glance* (1970) begins before a high prison
wall. On a white platform stands a tall, black woman in a dark, high-
collared dress, her back to the audience. To her right is a table, covered
with a white cloth, on which is placed a pitcher of milk, two glasses and
a knife. To her left is a child, who sits on a low white stool. Near him is
another child, apparently sleeping under a sheet. Moving extremely
slowly, the woman pours milk into a glass and takes it to the boy, who
drinks. She returns to the table, picks up the knife in her right hand,
wipes it, and moves to the boy again. She leans over him. He pays no
attention. Slowly, she stabs him. At this moment, Stefan Brecht observes
in his meticulous documentation of the piece:

> he collapses, she guides him down to the floor ... stabs him again,
> again very deliberately, carefully, in the back, withdraws the knife,
> walks back to the table, wipes off the knife again. Her action has been
> entirely unemotional.[62]

As she performs this act an older boy, Raymond Andrews, enters. He
stands and watches. At the same slow pace the woman pours another
glass of milk. She reveals a girl under the sheet and, waking her,
watches her drink. Replacing the glass on the table she collects the knife
and returns to the girl. As the girl sleeps the woman stabs her in the
same manner as the boy. This time, though, and when she stabs a second
time, Andrews makes the only sound he is capable of, 'a discontinuous
almost neuter scream, emotionally colourless jabs at utterance'.[63] The
woman returns to the table, wiping the knife. Finally, at the same pace,
she approaches the watching boy, whose scream becomes louder. Rather
than stabbing him the woman touches first his forehead, then his open
mouth, smothering his cry with a gesture of reassurance. The boy is
silent. The sequence takes up to a full hour to complete.

Presented at a pace she describes as approaching 'true slow motion ...
near-photographic time',[64] Sheryl Sutton's actions are such as to put into

question the nature and significance of the events she plays out. According to Stefan Brecht in *The Theatre of Visions: Robert Wilson* (Frankfurt am Main, 1978), such a mode of performance draws attention to itself as a possible source of meaning, and one which is in conflict with the expectations the events which it presents might normally raise. In his detailed record of the piece Brecht suggests that such acute slow-motion serves to make 'our experience ... pervasively dual: we are watching images and performers creating images.'[65]

For Wilson it would seem that the nature and pace of the performance serves to reveal complexities that normally remain unseen. In response to Ossia Trilling's enquiry as to the source or subject-matter of *KA MOUNTAIN AND GUARDenia TERRACE* (1972), Wilson recounted an experience evidently of great importance to him. Working for an anthropologist in New York in the 1960s, he made more than 300 films of mothers picking up and comforting their crying babies. Slowed down these films revealed that:

> when the baby's crying, in eight out of ten cases ... the initial reaction ... [is that] ... the mother is ... (a long, loud, low-pitched screech through the teeth) lunging at her baby. And the baby's responding with the body by (short screech, and grimace) fear, or many emotions simultaneously. Now, when we showed this film to the mother, she didn't believe it ... You see, we're not conscious. It's happening at another level, but with the body communicating in ways that sometimes we don't comprehend.[66]

Wilson's account offers a point from which the prologue to *Deafman Glance* may be read, and the scene has even been attributed directly to this experience. In *Robert Wilson and His Collaborators* (New York, 1989) Lawrence Shyer notes 'the maternal presence as the power of comfort (milk) and terror (knife)'.[67] Brecht observes that Sutton's gestures 'indicate a complete imbuement with a sense of maternal duty'.[68] Andrews's witnessing of the event can be read as a further play on these ambiguities. Here it is the witness to the event rather than the victim who is distressed, while his cry, which could speak for the children, the woman or the audience, is met by a gesture of reassurance.

Such a combination of elements, however, can also be related to the more complex implications of Wilson's anecdote. Wilson has suggested that the film demonstrates that 'the body doesn't lie ... we can trust the body'.[69] In this context, Wilson's story may suggest that when such actions are seen fully what they reveal is a great deal of complexity underlying apparently simple exchanges. It follows that the pace of Sutton's performance may be understood as an attempt to reveal ambiguities and raise questions that complicate a reading of her actions. Thus, the scene might not be so much a thematic exploration of 'motherhood' as a bringing into play of unexpected and multiple possibilities. The result is a performance which, in its development and despite its emotional power and resonance, resists the attempt to resolve images and sequences of images in terms of a particular meaning or meanings. It is from this point of view, of a resistance to a single resolution, that Sutton understands the effect of the figure she presents:

the character crosses so many cultural lines and periods. It's hard to say who it is. It's hard to say it's even a mother sometimes. She's a ritual figure. She might also be a priest – the black dress, the severe lines and the little white collar. Because the staging is so ritualistic, the murders seem almost religious. There are so many paradoxes, it's hard to define or delineate what you see. That's what makes it rich.[70]

The attempt to generate and sustain conflicting possibilities is evident too in the manner in which Wilson's large-scale performances unfold. In *Deafman Glance*, this first scene over, Andrews walks towards the wall which rises revealing 'a musical garden party on the old plantation'.[71] Music plays. A 'Black Mammy' dressed in white mimes playing a piano several inches above the keyboard. A dozen or so women sit listening to music, birds perched on the right hand of each. Nearby are an 'elegant waiting couple',[72] a young girl and an elderly gentleman. As the wall rises a 'pink angel' retreats and a stage-magician, dressed in top hat, tails and a cape, advances to the sound of piano chords. The murderess stops near the group of women. Andrews sits unobtrusively to one side of the stage. Now:

A grotesque outsider enters, destroying the reality of the plantation scene, a vulgar woman in a short, tight, cheap, worn, ill-fitting black dress, ankle boots and red socks, ridiculous black hat, with an awkwardly practical hand-bag attached to her stiffly sticking out arm.[73]

The newcomer writes in the air as if on an invisible surface. Another woman enters leading a live goat. Once the writing is complete the two make some kind of contact, then exit in different directions. The curtain gradually begins to fall. The murderess walks slowly towards the audience, then exits, followed by the waiting couple. The magician trails behind. The curtain down, the magician's motif announces the entry of a tall woman in a black dress. She is blindfolded. As she stands facing the wall, with one arm raised, the magician and his assistant remove the table, chairs and, finally, the corpses of the children. This done, the magician's assistant moves forward into a spotlight and announces the beginning of *Deafman Glance* which, he tells us, will last three hours. This he does 'in phoney, stage, ironic, demanding, weird tones, as though the play we are about to see was a play within some other play in which he was acting, a put-on: or a trick!'[74]

Here, while the parameters of the play are put into question, a process of extending and disrupting the various implications arising out of the murders has begun. The murderess has been followed out by the couple, who might take the place of the children, yet who never reappear as victims. The stance of the blindfolded woman echoes that of the murderess, yet she has entered to the magician's motif as if to take his place. The magician, in turn, gathers up the corpses and later, faintly in the distance, performs a wake for the dead children. As these sequences offer puzzling correspondences, individual images and actions are again put into question. Brecht, who performed in *The Life and Times of Sigmund Freud* (1969), *Overture to Ka Mountain* (1972) and *A Letter for Queen Victoria* (1974), suggests that 'the timing that holds a gesture the precise amount of time needed to make it sink in *and* make its mark is wrong in the Wilsonian performance: the Wilsonian performer either withdraws it as soon as it is being noticed ... or *holds* it until the spectator feels *exposed* to it.'[75]

As the piece proceeds, the juxtaposition of different kinds of performance also serves to fragment a sense of a formal coherence. While Raymond Andrews sits quietly and unself-consciously, the striking figure of the Black Mammy presents a deliberately exaggerated and self-conscious image, one which, Wilson suggests, is 'theatrical' and 'articulated as such'.[76] The awkward announcement of the play's beginning is strongly related to Wilson's own mode of performance, which Brecht describes as falling between a display of the difficulties of performing and bad acting.[77] Periodically, too, Wilson introduces actions and performers that seem out of place, presenting live animals or entirely inexperienced performers[78] who offer arbitrary and awkward presences which resist any easy incorporation into the developing actions and images.

Ironically, though, and despite such fragmentation, *Deafman Glance* continually alludes to the possibility of thematic and formal centres. As the piece progresses references to the child and murder are woven through the transforming and interlacing images. Andrews's continuous presence and the title itself may invite the idea that the piece is somehow the dream of the deaf boy or a meditation upon his mode of experiencing. The pattern into which these elements fall, however, serves only to stave off or complicate any particular thematic reading, as images and actions are placed in relationships which imply many possible and often competing significances.

This fragmentation and confusion of readings is fostered by Wilson's mode of composition. In his introduction to *The Life and Times of Sigmund Freud* (1969), originally presented as a prologue to its performance, Wilson set out his working method, which, despite any apparent subject-matter, involves an attention first of all to the formal and visual aspects of the presentation:

> the stage is divided into zones – stratified zones one behind the other ... in each of these zones there's a different 'reality' – a different activity defining the space so that from the audience's point of view one sees through these different layers, and as each occurs it appears as if there's been no realisation that anything other than itself is happening outside that particular designated area.[79]

In this way, elements are combined through an organising principle which, whatever correspondences it comes to imply between images and actions, has in its operation taken very little account of the thematic implication of any particular set or sequence of images. The resulting sense of dislocation is extended, too, in the repetition and variation of images through this process. Each image 'has a full register', meaning that 'at any point one element may be in full focus with all its parts together and later less or more of the parts are together'.[80] As a consequence not only thematic development but also the reading of role and conventional distinctions between performers tend to become confused. Observing his construction of *the CIVIL warS* (1984), Janny Donker notes the effect of Wilson's subordination of the actor to a developing formal logic:

> A role may ... be distributed among various actors, like a melody that is passed from one instrument to another. Conversely an actor may be playing various roles in succession – or even, from the viewpoint of the audience – simultaneously.[81]

In this context, the suggestion of a thematic key or centre, which in *Deafman Glance* has tended to be associated with Andrews's presence, is

typical of Wilson's work. Far from rejecting the possibility of such significances, Wilson builds his variations and sequences around highly
charged emotional, social and historical images. His performances have
embraced figures such as the King of Spain, Stalin, Queen Victoria, Einstein, Hess, Edison and Lincoln.[82] In each case, though, Wilson's mode of
composition has served to counter any simple articulation of the 'subject'
apparently at hand, while individual productions have had little to 'say' or
develop in connection with these figures. Wilson has also combined these
'historical' images and subject-matters in apparently arbitrary ways, and
certainly without regard to historical necessity. *The King of Spain* (1969)
was incorporated into *The Life and Times of Sigmund Freud* (1969),
becoming its second act, while in 1971 *Freud* was combined with
Deafman Glance to create a single 12-hour piece.

Wilson's use of language, too, follows a similar pattern, implying by
its presence logic and discourse while in its organisation confusing logical or discursive readings. Although in *Deafman Glance* language is
sparse, mostly conversational and constituted largely of *non sequiturs*, in
later productions such as *A Letter for Queen Victoria* (1974) and *The
Golden Windows* (1982), language is used extensively and Wilson has
published scripts.[83] Here, though, language seems to be organised
according to criteria that have little to do with its semantic properties. In
developing *A Letter for Queen Victoria* Wilson collaborated closely with
Christopher Knowles, who, like Wilson, was fascinated with pattern and
rhythm. According to Wilson, Knowles 'uses language as much for its
geometric structure as for its meaning. Sometimes he will take a word or
a phrase and build a structure out of it. He'll extend it to a pyramid or
some other shape and then reduce it back to a single phrase or letter ...
His constructions are very beautiful to look at. It's structured language.'[84]
A Letter for Queen Victoria is constructed out of such patterns in
which snatches of conversations are subjected to continual construction
and reconstruction according to rhythmic and visual schemes. The performers, of which Brecht was one, accepted this fragmentation, seeking
in performance to give their lines 'meanings independent of their literal
meanings'.[85] The result, Brecht argues, is a play which is primarily
visual and which offers 'the image of conversation, of different ways of
talking to each other'.[86]

Such paradoxes are fundamental to the effect of Wilson's work, where
formal correspondences between events and images draw attention and
give weight to juxtapositions and sequences that, thematically, have only
the most tendentious of connections. Through this Wilson offers a performance that repeatedly appears to articulate something in particular,

but which in fact presents images in ambiguous and ambivalent relationships to one another. Repeatedly, these performances invite readings of connections and parallels whose actual significances remain obscure. Consistently with this the performances are not generated out of any single scheme, while the subsequent sense of fragmentation is amplified by the independence of light and sound, including dialogue, which is often separated from its source and projected variously around the space.

In the context of such fragmentation, Wilson's choice of subject-matter is of great importance and takes its place alongside the work's more overtly formal strategies. Rather than articulating an historical subject-matter, Wilson's social and historical imagery can be read as serving an overtly formal function. Such images as these, by their very familiarity and emotional resonance, and so their formal weight as subject-matter, promise significance and invite readings. It is this 'formal weight' that Wilson exploits in his drawing of formal correspondences and equivalences across unlike and, seemingly, unrelated events and figures. It follows that the more socially significant or resonant the theme, the more effectively an audience might be drawn into the tensions that define the effect of the performance. Consistently with this, for Wilson the importance of figures such as Freud or Einstein would seem to lie not so much with the issues their presence might raise as their immediate resonance for an audience. Wilson has suggested that a research into the figures he uses would be counter productive to his work. In using the image of Einstein in *Einstein on the Beach* (1976), he stresses that 'I don't want to know any more about Einstein than what everyone knows about Einstein. I just want to know what the man in the street knows because that's what they'll bring to the work.'[87] Wilson's account of his treatment of the theme of *the CIVIL warS* (1984) similarly reflects not so much a concern with social, historical or political import as formal function, an elaboration of images which serves to set one thing against another while staving off particular conclusions. In *the CIVIL warS*, then, the way Frederick the Great relates to his father:

> could be a civil war. How the soldier puts his sock on before marching off into battle is a civil war; even a child learning to tie his shoe could be a civil war. It can be a situation like we have in Beirut today where there is no difference between civilians and soldiers.[88]

Such a gradual transformation and development of images which reflect and fold into each other as the piece progresses continually invites and at the same time seeks to displace particular readings. At a formal level, Wilson seems to understand his work as inviting or provoking a mode of seeing which might accept such conflicting and separate elements, each of which may be seen through or against each other. So, Wilson suggests, in its performance, *Freud* offers:

> a collage of different realities occurring simultaneous[ly] like being aware of several visual factors and how they combine into a picture before your eyes at any given moment. Awareness in that way occurs mostly through the course of experience of each layer rendering the others transparent.[89]

Such a process serves to put into question familiar objects, actions and events, where the attempt to read meaning and significance into emerging correspondences and patterns is deflected by multiple possibilities and implications. Here the act of reading itself becomes part of the subject-matter of the work, as meaning becomes multiple and elusive, constantly a possibility but always seeming out of reach. In his influential review of *Freud*, Richard Foreman emphasised the importance to Wilson's work of multiplicity and uncertainty. Fundamental to this work and its importance, he argues, is 'a sweet and powerful "placing" of various found and invented stage objects and actions – so placed and interwoven as to "show" at each moment as many of the implications and multi-level relations between objects and effects as possible.'[90]

At one level, this work seems impervious to 'reading'. Yet Wilson's presentations continually call attention to a developing play and parallel of resonant and familiar images, and so to a promise of purpose and significance. In this way, the work negotiates with the *act* of reading, but does so in order to stave off or deflect the attempt to close any particular reading and so arrive at any final, single or unself-conscious conclusion.

Against depth

Like the minimalist object, such performances resist the effort to penetrate the surface of the work, frustrating the reading of structure, sequence, pattern and image. In doing so, they mark out a fundamental opposition to the desire for *depth*, for the discovery of a 'centre' from whose vantage point the various elements which are presented may be understood. For Foreman such 'depth' is, unequivocally, 'the ultimate fantasy':

The ultimate evasion. Linked, of course, to a concept of centre. So de-
centre. Displace. Allow thought to float up from the depths and rest
on the surface.[91]

Not only Foreman but also Kirby and Wilson bring strategies into
play which move to reflect the viewer's attention back from a surface or
which displaces attention from one surface to another. While *Pandering
to the Masses* persistently and immediately denies its elements those
functions and purposes they promise to bring into play, *First Signs of
Decadence* offers 'realism' as a self-conscious construction, one whose
conventions are made visible through their arbitrary repetition and patterning. *Deafman Glance* presents a series of transforming surfaces
which would displace the attention from one image to another both
simultaneously and in sequence. While Foreman's presentations undermine the attempt to read meaning from moment to moment, Kirby and
Wilson's work invites multiple and conflicting readings. Even the promise of meaning, here, is shifting and unstable, while the desire to discover meanings, the promise of which these pieces invariably play with,
is always frustrated. What remains is a play of prompts, of indications or
traces which displace one other, a de-centring which continually staves
off a final closure.

In this way, all three of these pieces exemplify a resistance to that
totality which would be definitively *meaningful*. Through shifting and
self-reflexive strategies the notion that meaning can somehow *belong* to
the 'work', that its elements can be understood as *possessing* its meaning, is directly challenged. These performances, one can argue, look
above all towards the 'event' which occurs between the spectator and the
presentation, an 'event' made visible both by the resistance to depth and
the deflection between and across surfaces and signifying elements. Such
a refutation of the properly meaningful amounts to an attack not only on
the autonomy of the work of art but the specularity of the sign, as the
attempt to read, to discover depth, is persistently deflected, de-centred,
thrown back upon itself, in an exposure of the contingency of the 'work'
and that which the viewer discovers in the moment of its presentation.

Chapter 4

Modern Dance and the Modernist Work

In performance theory and criticism the use of the term 'postmodern' has had its longest history in association with the changes in American dance of the early 1960s. Like the modern architectural styles against which Charles Jencks sets his description of the postmodern in art, the rejection of a self-consciously modern and stylised American dance by the dancers and artists associated with the Judson Dance Theater in New York has been taken to mark a radical departure from 'modern' modes of work. After Clement Greenberg's account of the modernist project, influential readings of the modern, the modernist and, consequently, the postmodern in performance have been constructed around the Judson Dance Theater's rejection of the expressionism characteristic of modern choreographies. In the context of Michael Fried's unequivocal condemnation of the 'theatrical' in art, however, one might challenge the very possibility of a properly 'modernist' performance, and, in turn, these readings of the move from a modern and to a postmodern dance.

From modern to postmodern dance

As it came to be defined in the work of Martha Graham, Doris Humphrey, her partner Charles Wiedman and the German-born dancer Hanya Holm, American modern dance had its roots in the rejection of the conventional languages of classical dance and an exploration of the

71

expressive properties of movement and compositional pattern. In his book with Carroll Russell, *Modern Dance Forms* (San Francisco, 1961), which drew on Graham's method and recorded his own influential teaching, Graham's partner and musical director, Louis Horst, stressed the importance of the modern dance's rejection not only of the formal strictures of the classical tradition but also the 'free dance' inspired by Isadora Duncan. Arguing that modern dance had turned away from both 'the dry technicalities of ballet and the vague formlessness of "interpretative" dance',[1] Horst saw Graham and her contemporaries as rediscovering the expressive function of dance through an address to the essentials of choreographic form.

Yet despite Horst's injunction against Duncan's romanticism and Graham's own dismissal of the 'weakling exoticism'[2] of Ruth St Denis and Ted Shawn, the work of this second generation of modern dancers had its roots firmly within that which it ostensibly rejected. Most obviously, the work of Graham, Humphrey and Wiedman was born directly out of a reaction against the Denishawn Company, with whom they had been associated until as late as 1923. Evidently, too, the formal innovations of St Denis and Shawn, among others including Loie Fuller and Maud Allen,[3] acted as a spur to this second generation of dancers' revitalised concern with form. At the same time, and despite Horst's rejection of her pursuit of the spontaneous, Isadora Duncan's understanding of the unity of choreographic and musical composition, her desire to discover languages natural to the body and so direct in their communication, and her notion of the dance's unique embodiment of feeling, find themselves echoed in the new generation's assumption of the expressive function of dance.

Building on these earlier departures, this second wave of modern dance was characterised not only by a concern for form but an assumption that the identity of dance as an art must be bound up with the expressive power and significance of dance-movement. So while Doris Humphrey grounded her compositional method in what she saw as the fundamental properties of dance-movement and pattern,[4] for her the key to the modern remained that of 'working from the inside out ... it's the dominant expression of our generation, if not of the age'.[5] Graham, similarly, understood dance to be an externalisation in which the acting out of an 'interior landscape' was bound up with the formal properties of dance as a medium. The expressive function of dance was not simply something marked out by style or intent, but was to be discovered within its very form, as an inherent property of movement. Graham notes:

Dance is another way of putting things. It isn't a literal or literary thing, but everything that a dancer does, even in the most lyrical thing, has a definite and prescribed meaning. If it could be said in words, it would be; but outside of words, outside of painting, outside of sculpture, *inside* the body is an interior landscape which is revealed in movement.[6]

For Susan Foster, in her book *Reading Dancing* (Berkeley, Cal., 1986), this understanding of dance as the externalisation of inner, subjective but universal truths defines an expressionism which embraces the work of modern dancers from Duncan through to Graham and a subsequent third and fourth generation of choreographers. At the same time, and as a part of this expressionism, Foster understands the continuity of modern dance to lie in the very process of rejection and re-invention of movement vocabularies. Rather than build upon prevailing languages of dance, she suggests, the second generation of modern dancers rejected the work of their teachers, and often their contemporaries, as a testimony to the validity and seriousness of their own artistic impulses. Thus, the very fact that 'one person chose the subject-matter of the dance, invented the vocabulary to express that subject, and then danced the final composition' served only to heighten its 'immediacy and authenticity'.[7]

In the consolidation of American modern dance after the war, however, the emphasis upon the fundamental properties of form and the techniques and compositional methods understood to reveal those properties came to the fore. Both Horst's *Modern Dance Forms* and Doris Humphrey's *The Art of Making Dances* (New York, 1959) emphasise formal compositional problems and look towards the essentials of choreographic method and so the parameters of movement vocabulary. Horst, aligning the Graham technique to the modern styles of art, even stresses the absolute nature and continuity of the laws of composition. Drawing attention to the 'fundamental rules' of form he states categorically that 'composition is based on only two things: a conception of a theme and the manipulation of that theme, whatever the chosen theme may be, it cannot be manipulated, developed, shaped, without knowledge of the rules of composition'.[8] Such a manipulation, he argues, should also follow certain basic patterns which underlie all artistic composition and which include 'theme and variation', the 'Rondo' and 'the most deeply instinctual aesthetic form ... the ABA'.[9] Here art even takes up:

the universal pattern of life itself: we are born, we live, we return to the unknown. It is the *three part form* which is the rhythm of the natural drumbeat, the pattern of the common limerick verse, and also the usual basis of serious musical composition, from a single song to a complex symphony.[10]

In Horst's work, particularly, but also through the pervasive influence of the Graham and Humphrey schools on the teaching of dance, this consolidation came to look towards the circumscription of a vocabulary of means. It is as a rejection of this prevailing understanding of dance in terms of a particular expressive function, of appropriate styles and materials, and so of a limited range of methods and patterns of composition, that Sally Banes defines a specifically 'post-modern' performance in her influential book *Terpsichore in Sneakers: Post-modern Dance* (Boston, Mass., 1980). In the work of the Judson Dance Theater presented between 1962 and 1964, in particular, Banes identifies a break away from the work of modern choreographers and the emergence of new attitudes and styles of work that define a range of specifically postmodern departures.

Defining postmodern dance

Although Merce Cunningham had introduced chance into his compositional method as early as 1951, and had worked with the composer John Cage since 1942, by the late 1950s the assumptions and practices of expressionist dance still prevailed in non-classical teaching and practice. Cunningham himself had been a principal dancer in Graham's company, while many of Cunningham's own company had trained in the modern dance methods defined by Humphrey, Graham and Horst. Of the 15 dancers and artists who showed work in the first concert of dance presented at the Judson Church in June 1962, Steve Paxton, Ruth Emerson, William Davis, Judith Dunn and David Gordon, each of whom had been associated with the Cunningham company, had all trained in the Graham technique or taken classes with Louis Horst. Robert Dunn, whose classes in choreography at the Cunningham studio between 1960 and 1962 had given rise to the Judson Dance Theater's first concerts, went so far as to set his interest in chance method against Horst's concern for the expressive function of music and the close correspondence of musical and choreographic composition. In a similar vein, Dunn set the openness of his classes against the 'oppressive' nature of Horst's teaching, suggesting, in an interview with Sally Banes, that 'if indeed I helped liberate people from Louis [Horst] and Doris

[Humphrey] (who was a great woman, but still) ... that was well worth doing'.[11] In fact, the eclecticism of Dunn's teaching served to challenge the very notion of 'appropriate' function and form. Rather than pursue any particular idea of the nature or purpose of dance, Dunn looked towards other disciplines, using his classes as a 'clearinghouse for structures derived from various sources of contemporary action: dance, music, painting, sculpture, Happenings, literature'.[12] In her detailed record of the Judson concerts, *Democracy's Body: Judson Dance Theater, 1962–1964* (Ann Arbor, Mich., 1983), Banes identifies just such an exchange between disciplines with a sensibility underlying the Judson work as a whole:

> Perhaps even more important than the individual dances given at a Judson concert was the attitude that anything might be called a dance and looked at as a dance; the work of a visual artist, a filmmaker, a musician might be considered a dance, just as activities done by a dancer, although not recognizable as theatrical dance, might be re-examined and 'made strange' because they were framed as art.[13]

Such an eclecticism and sense of a liberation from prevailing assumptions is evident, too, in the sheer variety of departures that characterised the Judson concerts. Banes observes that the work of the Judson Dance Theater embraced the 'baroque style' of David Gordon, Fred Herko and Aileen Rothlein, a form of multi-media performance exemplified in aspects of Elaine Summers's and Judith Dunn's work as well as the 'analytic, reductive' performances with which it is often associated. Even here Banes sees distinct and contrasting styles:

> Yvonne Rainer's dialectical work, mixing ordinary or grotesque movement with traditional dance techniques ... Steve Paxton's fusion of nature and culture, his framing of mundane actions like eating and walking ... Robert Morris' task dances, using objects to focus the attention of both performer and audience and his references within works to other artworks ... Lucinda Childs' cool performance style, rooted first in the handling of objects and later in pure movement structures; Trisha Brown's improvisations and flyaway movements.[14]

For Banes, though, while the Judson Dance Theater defines itself as 'historically post-modern' in its break from expressionist modes of choreography, its work represents a phase of dance in which fundamental aspects of *modernism* come to the fore, as the theatrical style and

emotional content of expressionist choreographies are rejected in favour
of a more exclusive focus upon form. Suggesting that the term 'postmodern' 'means something different in every art form', Banes argues in
her introduction to the second edition of *Terpsichore in Sneakers*
(Middleton, Conn., 1987) that 'in dance, the confusion the term "postmodern" creates is further complicated by the fact that historical modern
dance never really was *modernist*'.[15] In seeking to strip movement of
'expression', in doing away with choreography's tie to music and narrative, the dancers and artists associated with the Judson concerts are
understood by Banes to have pursued a modernist aesthetic analogous to
that which Greenberg proposes for modernist painting. It follows that
the resultant pared-down or 'minimal' dance might properly be considered at once 'post-modern', in the sense of an open reaction against a
self-styled modern American dance, and yet *modernist* in its stripping
away of that which is 'unessential' to dance as a medium.

Important as it is, however, Banes's reading raises both historical and
theoretical questions concerning the possible relationships between
modern, modernist and a postmodern dance. Historically, one can argue
that a description of 'post-modern' dance as modernist involves a separating out of certain Judson presentations from work with which it seems
to interpenetrate and yet which is not consistent with Greenberg's
project. Robert Rauschenberg, for example, extended his work directly
into the realm of performance through a participation in nine of the six-
teen Judson concerts. Robert Morris, whose minimal sculptures Michael
Fried later pronounced to be antithetical to the modernist work, regularly presented performances with the Judson group and, later, under the
aegis of Fluxus. The dancer Simone Forti and the artist Carolee Schneemann performed both within the Judson Dance Theater and as members
of the Fluxus group.[16] Yvonne Rainer and Aileen Rothlein of the Judson
group both performed in Schneemann's *Environment for Sound and
Motions* in a concert organised by Philip Corner and Dick Higgins in
May 1962, shortly before the first of the Fluxus and Judson Church concerts. In this way, the participation of many of the Judson Church dancers in the YAM festival of May 1963, which brought together
Happenings, Fluxus, new music and dance, and which was organised by
George Brecht and Robert Watts, can be read as part of a wider
exchange of ideas, practices and presentations.[17]

More fundamentally, though, the very notion that, after Greenberg, a
'reduction' of dance to movement without regard to representation or
expression, or even to the presence of the dancer alone, constitutes a
projection toward a legitimating essence needs to be put into question.

After Greenberg, Fried emphasises the difficulty theatre has in so far as it aspires to the modernist ideal. Like music, he argues, theatre is durational and, like any performance, 'theatre *has* an audience – it *exists for* one – in a way the other arts do not'.[18] For Fried, then, 'this more than anything else is what modernist sensibility finds intolerable in theatre generally'.[19] Fried's charge challenges not simply the analogy between modernist painting and 'post-modern' dance, but the very prospect of a properly modernist programme within performance.

Modern dance and the modernist work

In considering a modernist dance after Greenberg, one can begin either by addressing, as Banes does, coincidences with non-objective art and so between a 'post-modern' dance and that abstract painting Greenberg privileges, or critical and theoretical readings of dance as an autonomous aspect of art. In the first instance one begins with the morphology and development of the work, in the second one might look towards a theoretical ground and a reading of dance animated by assumptions close to Greenberg's own. Yet in addressing readings of dance as a formally unique and self-legitimating medium, one not only returns to criticism and theory bound up with modernism, but to assumptions and ideas which are coincident in various ways with the practice of 'modern' rather than 'post-modern' choreographers. Indeed, and ironically, in taking this route through theory and criticism, one can return to presentations that have little to do with non-objective art; in fact, to 'historical modern dance' itself.

In *Reading Dancing* Susan Foster observes that the three most influential theories of dance composition, formulated by the ethnologist Curt Sachs, the critic John Martin and the philosopher Suzanne K. Langer, all 'locate the origins of dance in early human gestural attempts at communication'.[20] In doing so, she notes, 'they oppose these primal yearnings to express human feeling to the subsequent artificiality of civilised movement, and they look to dance as a medium that can return us to a vital energy and an unalienated sense of wholeness'.[21] For Sachs and Martin modern dance, specifically, is characterised by an attempt to rediscover this vitality, and so implicitly obtains a special place and purpose with regard to the nature and function of dance, as it projects itself toward the foundations of the medium.

Writing in his *World History of the Dance* (New York, 1937), Sachs argues that both Duncan's break from classical convention and the popularity of 'American Negro and Creole dances' signalled a rediscovery of the body and a desire to return to the fundamental sources of dance. In doing so, he suggests, modern dance sought a new authenticity:

> Our generation does not find what it seeks in ballet ... It cries out, as Noverre once did, for nature and passion; again it desires, as he did, though perhaps too strongly, to exchange stereotyped movement for something genuinely of the soul.[22]

Martin, who, unlike Sachs, specifically sought to theorise the moderns' practice, argues similarly in his *Introduction to the Dance* (New York, 1939) that Duncan's work should be understood as 'a profound overturning, clearing away ages of accumulation of intellectual restraints and yielding the power of motion to the inner man'.[23] In doing so, Martin supposes, modern dance seeks not only its own origins but that of art itself, for 'the medium in which the art impulse first expresses itself is that of movement'.[24]

This primitivism, which Robert Goldwater traces widely throughout European modernism in *Primitivism in Modern Art* (London, 1938), was self-conscious in the work of modern dancers themselves. In 1931 Graham's celebrated *Primitive Mysteries* employed Christian imagery and ritual forms drawn from her studies of North American Indians, while Humphrey's *Shakers* of the same year incorporated studies of ecstatic religious worship. Similarly, and drawing on Graham's practice, Horst points toward the 'elemental nature' of the impulse to dance and the 'deep responsiveness between body and mind'[25] out of which he believed the art of dance was formed. Dance, in Horst's view, carries within it this aspect of the primitive and the essential, as if to remind us that '[t]housands of years of civilisation have endowed us moderns with only a veneer of refinement to separate us from our crude and naive ancestors'.[26]

Importantly, too, in their association of the sources of dance with pre-verbal, non-intellectual impulses, these ideas speak not only of the special significance of dance as a medium but of the difficulty of discussing the actual significances of any particular dance. In this way, again, Sachs, Martin and Langer participate in a critical modernism, finding themselves on common ground with self-consciously modern practitioners in their assumptions about the dance's special and defining qualities. For these critics, Foster suggests, 'as for the majority of early twentieth century choreographers ... the dance functions as a luminous

symbol of unspeakable human truths, which, because they are unspeakable, leave us with little to say about the dance's organisation'.[27]

The notion that dance reveals a 'special' significance, however,
serves not only to set it apart from a criticism which is unable to represent that which the 'art-dance' articulates, but also from other genres
of art. Indeed, in considering the nature and importance of such 'significance' these accounts of dance look toward those qualities which make
dance 'distinct', which, in fact, embody what is unique to it as an artistic
medium. In this respect, what emerges from a close reading of Langer
and Martin's theorising of dance, as opposed to Sachs more broadly
historical approach, is an understanding of the 'art-dance' as a self-
determining work of art, existing in its own aesthetic realm, and a corresponding conception of how the medium of dance legitimates itself *as
a fine art*. In elaborating these ideas, one might first address Langer's
comprehensive theory of art and performance and, in this context,
Martin's detailed address to the nature of modern dance.

Suzanne Langer begins her address to the fundamental characteristics of art by reviewing the body of ideas upon which she builds. In the
work that precedes her own, Langer argues, the key concerns and questions of aesthetic theory 'all converge on the same problem: what is
significant in art? What, in other words, is meant by "Significant
Form"?'[28] As this question implies, Langer assumes at her point of
departure that 'significance' is a property of artistic form; that the vital
import and so the qualities by which the work of art is defined reside,
definitively, *within* it. In *Feeling and Form: A Theory of Art* (London,
1953), Langer emphasises the necessity of looking 'upon the art object
as something in its own right, with properties independent of our prepared reactions – properties which command our reactions, and make it
the autonomous and essential factor it is in every human culture'.[29] It is
on this basis, too, that Langer understands art and critical discourse to
be entirely separate and distinct. Indeed, Langer defines 'significance'
in art by opposing it to the nature of meaning in language, producing,
through this opposition, an account of the function and effect of the
work of art.

Accepting the transparency of language, Langer argues that the elementary unit of language exists on the basis of a simple and conventionally fixed correlation between a word or combination of words and a
given object or idea. So far as such 'associative symbols' are concerned,
meaning is fixed and straightforward. In the operation of language, however, and where such symbols are used in combination, meaning, and so
the symbol itself, become more complex. In a sentence, she notes,

meaning is expressed through the organisation of associative symbols rather than through the value of the symbols alone. Here, 'one may say that the elements of propositions are *named* by words, but propositions themselves are *articulated* by sentences'.[30] It follows that a sentence, which is a 'complex symbol', can properly be described as an 'articulate form', where meaning is found through the perception of its internal structure rather than simply through the presence and value of its constituent elements.

It is after this model that Langer characterises the symbolic nature of art, a nature which she first sets out in *Philosophy in a New Key* (Cambridge, Mass., 1942) in her special theory of music. Like a complex symbol in language, Langer observes, a musical composition is an 'articulate form':

> Its parts not only fuse together to yield a greater entity, but in so doing they maintain some degree of separate existence, and the sensuous character of each element is affected by its function in the complex whole. This means that the greater entity we call a composition is not merely produced by mixture, like a new colour made by mixing paints, but is *articulated* ... .[31]

Yet music is fundamentally different from language, for its constituent elements, what would be the associative symbols, do not make fixed and specific reference to any idea or object. Thus while language is pre-eminently logical and intellectual, music, which presents itself as pattern without conventional reference, cannot possess rational significance and is an analogue of experience as it is felt rather than understood. The corollary of this is not simply that art and criticism lie in separate and distinct realms, but that the formal terms by which the work of art is constituted and the nature of the significance art has to offer are bound one within the other. Thus, one can say definitively that the work of art *is* an analogue of sensual and emotional experience. In elaborating this model of art as an 'articulate but non-discursive form', Langer not only defines an opposition between art and language, but, in describing the self-determination of the work of art, oppositions between the 'significant form' that announces the work and its literal contexts as well as the various genres of art.

Within Langer's conception of art as an 'articulate form', the identity of the work of art cannot be understood simply in terms of the individual elements of which it is constituted. Instead, it is 'significant form', arising through the *articulation* of physical elements, that announces the work of art. It follows from this that, in the most fundamental sense, the work of art comes into being at the point at which it separates itself from the material elements upon which it is reliant, at the point at which it establishes itself as an 'illusion', a 'virtual object'. Langer emphasises the importance of this distinction, observing that the 'illusion, which constitutes the work of art, is not a mere arrangement of given materials in an aesthetically pleasing pattern; it is what results from the arrangement, and is literally something the artist makes, not something he finds'.[32] It follows that at the very heart of the work of art is an abstraction, a separateness from the material environment that surrounds it, even a separateness from the physical object without which it could not exist. Langer emphasises the importance of the 'air of illusion, of being a sheer image' that she associates with the work of art, noting:

Every real work of art has a tendency to appear thus dissociated from its mundane environment. The most immediate impression it creates is one of 'otherness' from reality – the impression of an illusion enfolding the thing, action, statement, or flow of sound that constitutes the work.[33]

Nor is this effect produced by the way in which the work is seen or understood by the viewer. Arguing that the work of art constitutes itself by this very 'detachment from reality',[34] Langer emphasises that 'it is not the percipient who discovers the surroundings, but the work of art which, if it is successful, detaches itself from the rest of the world; he merely sees it as it is presented to him'.[35] In these terms, and coincidentally with Fried, the successful work of art can be said, by its very nature, to effect not only a separation of itself from its mundane environment but a transcendence of its own objecthood.

It is in the context of this autonomy, this separation of the definition and qualities of the work from the 'literal' materials and circumstances upon which it is dependent, that Langer makes her distinctions between the various modes of art. If the fundamental condition of art is one of abstraction, it follows that the identities of the various forms of art may lie in the particular nature of the abstraction of which they consist. Thus, Langer argues, each 'art gender' is defined by its own 'primary illusion', its own 'virtual realm' consisting of 'the basic creation wherein all its elements exist' and which, in turn, its elements 'produce and support'.[36] By their very natures, each of these realms is separated both from the material contexts in which the work of art is found and any other virtual realm. The absolute nature of this distinction, and of the work's separation of itself from its mundane environment, is demonstrated in Langer's account of the primary illusion of the plastic arts. Langer begins by setting out what she takes to be the formal function of this particular mode of art:

> The purpose of all plastic art is to articulate visual form, and to present that form ... as the sole or at least paramount, object of perception. This means that for the beholder the work of art must be not only a shape in space, but a shaping *of* space – of all the space that he is given.[37]

For Langer this means that the treatment of space within the plastic arts is quite removed from our experience of space in life. While we perceive objects in relation to one another in space, 'space' as we experience it over time and through our various senses, Langer suggests, cannot be said to have 'shape' for it has no 'concrete totality'.[38] It follows that the 'picture space' which is defined in the plastic arts is not an articulation of space as we experience it in life at all, but of a created virtual space, an illusory space 'that exists for vision alone'.[39] Not only this, but by its very nature as an illusion, virtual space has a discontinuous relationship with practical space and so with the literal contexts in which the work of art presents itself. Langer observes:

> Being visual this space has no continuity with the space in which we live; it is limited by the frame or by the surrounding blanks, or incongruous things that cut it off. Yet its limits cannot even be said to *divide* it from practical space; for a boundary that divides things always connects things as well, and between a picture space and any other space there is no connection. The created virtual space is entirely self-contained and independent.[40]

The autonomous nature of this primary illusion also establishes a fundamental distinction between any work that articulates virtual space and any work whose primary illusion lies in another virtual realm. Just as 'everything that is relevant and artistically valid in a picture must be visual',[41] so whatever elements enter into a piece of music must find a place and a function within its primary illusion of 'virtual time'. In turn, Langer notes, the primary illusion of poetry is that of 'virtual life'; of drama, 'virtual future'. Dance, similarly, establishes itself through its own unique abstraction; that of gesture, drawn out of its practical contexts so that it may enter into the symbolic realm of art. Langer observes that 'dance gesture is not real gesture, but virtual ... it is *actual movement*, but *virtual self-expression*'.[42] On this basis Langer's understanding of the symbol in art allows her to reveal dance's basic abstraction and its primary illusion, that of the 'virtual realm of Power':

> Every being that makes natural gestures is a centre of a vital force, and its expressive movements are seen by others as signals of its will. The spontaneously gestic character of dance motions is illusory, and the vital force they express is illusory; the powers (ie: centres of vital force) in dance are created beings – created by the semblance gesture.[43]

In this way, each art is necessarily defined by that virtual realm which is its primary illusion and in which it, alone, exists. It is a realm that is entirely self-contained and self-supporting, a realm that, like the work itself, is autonomous. So, Langer concludes, 'a work never belongs to more than one realm, and it always establishes that one completely and immediately as its very substance'.[44]

It follows that not only does Langer's theory assert the autonomy of the work of art, its transcendence of its material conditions and even its own objecthood, but it also proposes an absolute distinction between the various forms of art and what is proper to them. Therefore, Langer concludes, a recognition of the virtual realm of dance finally allows a proper consideration of what is unique to dance, and offers a solution to common confusions in both dance criticism and practice over what is and is not truly appropriate to the medium. Thus:

> The recognition of a true artistic illusion, a realm of 'Powers' ... lifts the concept of dance out of all its theoretical entanglements with music, painting, comedy and carnival or serious drama, and lets one ask *what belongs to dancing*, and what does not.[45]

Clearly, Langer's theory does not specifically look towards the legitimation of the modernist programme Greenberg elaborates. Indeed, Langer explicitly rejects such a programme for art and sees no necessary connection between the abstraction she takes to be the fundamental condition of art and a modernist projection towards the formal essence of the work of art. Langer states categorically that 'abstract form as such is not an artistic ideal. To carry abstraction as far as possible, and achieve pure form in only the barest conceptual medium, is a logician's business, not a painter's or poet's.'[46]

At the same time, though, this theorising of the work's possession of its own meaning and identity and of the necessary and unbridgeable separation of 'art-genders' enters into a concept of the work of art with which Greenberg's modernist project participates. Like Langer, both Greenberg and Fried argue for the immanence of the work; its inherent significance, its necessary separation from its material conditions, its transcendence of its own objecthood. Indeed, unless the work of art is understood as imbued with qualities entirely its own, unless it can be seen as standing apart from its 'mundane environment', self-possessed and self-sufficient in an autonomous realm, then a projection towards those qualities which lie definitively *within* the work cannot make sense. It follows that while Langer's theory does not seek to define a modernist art or dance, it nevertheless rehearses assumptions essential to the modernist programme.

While it is on this ground that Langer's understanding of art intersects with Greenberg's notion of the modernist work, it is here, too, that her conception of art crosses with John Martin's analysis of the function and character of modern dance. This is not to imply that these theories and practices should be collapsed one into the other, but simply that their coincident assumptions mark out a ground which this idea of the modernist work assumes and depends upon. It is on this ground, then, that one can look towards ways in which Greenberg's understanding of modernist painting crosses with a reading of historical modern dance.

In defining dance as 'the expression, by means of bodily movement arranged in significant form, of concepts which transcend the individual's power to express by rational and intellectual means',[47] John Martin accords in general with Langer's assumptions about the character and function of art. More specifically, in this context, Martin understands the emergence of modern dance to signal a return to the proper purpose and nature of 'dance as a fine art';[48] that is, the expression through appropriately 'significant', rather than conventional or codified, forms, of 'extra-intellectual' and so ineffable meaning.

In his account of the history and development of modern dance, Martin points first to its fulfilment of romantic ideals; its rejection of the 'artifice' of the inherited languages of classical ballet and its chief aim, which it shares with romanticism, of 'the expression of an inner compulsion'.[49] Yet it is precisely here, too, that for Martin modern dance departs from the more problematic assumptions of romanticism and, in particular, from romantic attitudes toward composition in a distinct and defining 'realisation of the aesthetic value of form'.[50] Where romantic or 'free dance', with its emphasis upon spontaneous expression, Martin supposes, threatens to confuse artistic significance with 'self-expression', the modern dance concerns itself directly with the creation of compositional forms which possess and articulate 'significance'. In this way, Martin argues, modern dance defines itself in opposition to the 'decadence' of classical ballet while transcending the naive aspects of the romantic movement and, in doing so, looks toward the fundamental character of dance as an art-form. Indeed, Martin understands the projection toward a marriage of expressive function and significant form as a projection toward a realisation of the defining principles underlying the medium itself. Here modern dance not only takes up the proper function of dance as a fine art but, in an explicitly modernist mode, looks towards its fundamental and legitimating characteristics as a discipline.

Clarifying this critical aspect of modern dance in *The Modern Dance* (New York, 1933), Martin considers its four principal discoveries. The first of these emerges at the point at which modern dance defines itself as distinct from romanticism and where movement itself, as an independent entity, is understood to lie at the core of dance as an artistic medium. Here, Martin argues, rather than employing movement as a means of animating and unifying a highly conventional vocabulary of attitudes and poses, or allowing movement to arise spontaneously from an intense focus upon the dancer and the inspirational effect of music, modern dance takes movement itself to be the essence of dance and the key to its significance. This is not simply to say that all dance consists of movement, but rather that movement is what is significant in dance; that movement is the very substance of dance and literally the site of its meaning.

Out of this arises the second discovery. Asserting that as 'the most elementary physical experience of human life'[51] no movement of the body can ever be entirely non-representational or meaningless, Martin argues that the kinaesthetic response to movement, the sympathetic muscular response of the spectator to the impulse of the dancer, is inevitably complimented by a psychical response of some kind; an image, idea or a feeling. This being the case, Martin concludes, movement, as such, is by its nature *significant*. It follows that, just as it is only with the advent of modern dance that movement is understood to be the substance of dance, it is only with the emergence of modern dance that this 'metakinesis' can come fully into play as a compositional element. This is not to say that this process has not always been important to the nature and effect of theatrical dance, but rather that in modern dance, through its isolation of movement, this essential property becomes fully available to the artist. So Martin states categorically that 'no conscious artistic use was made of metakinesis until the modern dance arose'.[52]

Having concluded that movement itself is the substance of dance and that all movement is inherently significant, it follows that the 'substance' or 'material' properly appropriate to dance is 'continuous or sustained movement', movement that 'contains no static elements, no attitudes however decorative which might be considered points of rest'.[53] Hence the characteristic 'dynamism' of modern dance, in which 'there is never a moment in which the dancer lapses into natural physical rest'[54] represents an exclusion of elements unessential and so corruptive to dance as an art form.

Finally, Martin's assumption that movement is the site of meaning and that all movement has significance leads him to conclude that while 'compositional form' is inherently significant, no one form, or set of conventional forms, can circumscribe the possible vocabulary of dance. In fact it is the very freedom from conventional vocabularies that allows the modern dancer to employ the various properties of movement in an entirely appropriate way and, through this, to create compositional forms free of ornamentation and distraction which are appropriately expressive and significant. Martin emphasises that in modern dance 'each dance makes its own form'[55] and that in making its own form each successful dance will come to a unique 'significant form'. Here, again, Martin's understanding coincides with Langer's:

> Form ... is capable of operating of itself. It may, indeed, be the result of unifying diverse elements whereby they achieve collectively an aesthetic vitality which except by this association they would not possess. The whole thus becomes greater than the sum of its parts. This unifying process by which form is attained is known as composition.[56]

Although in *The Modern Dance* Martin does not use the term 'modernist', what he describes here is the self-conscious realisation within the work of art of the essential terms underlying the medium. In dance, he asserts, 'the leaders of the modern movement ... have succeeded in performing the greatest service to their art in discovering its essential substance and the dimension in which it exists'.[57] For Martin, and because rather than in spite of its expressionism, historical modern dance is taken to be a projection toward the 'essence' of dance as a medium which, at its height, promises to reveal the absolute dance, 'that pure essence of dancing which contains no element of anything else'.[58]

The object of dance

Martin's position does not simply reveal theoretical and critical coincidences between a reading of the modernist project in art and dance, but demonstrates the very difficulty of extending the model of a modernist autonomy into a reading of performance. Indeed, the juxtaposition of Langer, Martin and Banes's readings of dance against Greenberg's ideal of the self-legitimating work, reveals not simply a debate over the terms of a modernist performance, but the very resistance of 'theatre' to a realisation of a properly modernist programme.

Despite his assertion that movement is the substance of dance and that all movement has significance, Martin does not suppose that all movement is possible or suitable material for the 'art dance'. Indeed, he takes the modern dance's realisation of the essential properties of the medium to involve an exclusion of elements inappropriate to it as a fine art. Martin states categorically:

All movement ... is not suitable material for the creation of the dance. All dance is made of movement, but all movement is not dance; just as all music is sound, but all sound is not music; or all poetry is words, but all words are not poetry.[59]

In seeking to create 'significant form', Martin argues, the dancer must discard that movement which 'is the stuff of daily, routine physical living' and 'select the kind of movement that is not subordinate and subsidiary to physical necessity, but is the product of a mental, an emotional, or non-physical demand'.[60] In Martin's view such a distinction is essential to dance's definition of itself as an art-form. Martin even concludes that 'art and nature are irreconcilable opposites. For this reason natural movements and natural rhythms are impossible materials for the art dance'.[61]

Langer makes an analogous distinction. Here the 'work of art' is never something the artist finds or to which the spectator gives identity by the act of looking, but is something that has been *made* and which asserts *its own* identity as art. It follows that a dance is never simply 'movement', but is always movement that has been transformed, movement that has been 'imagined', remade and made 'articulate'. With regard to dance, Langer argues:

Gesticulation, as part of our actual behaviour, is not art. It is simply movement. A squirrel, startled, sitting up with its paws against its

heart, makes a gesture, and a very expressive one at that. But there is
no art in its behaviour. It is not dancing. Only when the movement
that was a genuine gesture in the squirrel is *imagined*, so it may be
performed apart from the squirrel's momentary situation and mental-
ity, can it become an artistic element, a possible dance gesture.[62]

The autonomous work of art makes its nature clear by an absolute differentiation of itself, by properties which are its own, from the mundane
circumstances in which it presents itself. For the 'art dance', this self-
determination necessarily involves a differentiation of 'the dance' from
'movement-in-general'. Hence Martin's antipathy toward 'everyday'
movement and 'natural' rhythms. For Martin, as for Langer, dance
cannot be merely 'movement', but is necessarily a movement or pattern
of movement which has set itself apart from movement-in-general by
what it *is*. Such movement is not defined as 'art' by a contingent set of
circumstances or contexts, for it creates its own context, differentiating
itself from that which is around it. Here there can be no confusion
between the 'art dance' and everyday movement, because the art dance
is in possession of its own identity as art. Indeed, Greenberg's reading of
the projection of the modernist work toward those terms which are
definitively *within* it, is a reading of the work of art as an uncovering of
precisely such a self-determination.

The significance of this becomes clearer when it is set against the
model of historical postmodern dance. For Sally Banes it is the reduction
of dance to simply the presentation of 'movement', even taking the form
of a simple functional task, that defines historical postmodern dance as
modernist. Yet where 'dance' is understood to be differentiated from
'movement-in-general' only by the fact of its presentation to an audience,
then the very notion of a self-determination is threatened. Movement
defined as dance by how it is *framed* and, therefore, by how it is *seen*, is
not self-determining in the way Langer, Martin and Greenberg suppose
that the work of art must be. In fact, in Fried's terms, such a challenge to
the differentiation of the work of art from its mundane circumstances,
including the circumstances of its presentation, can only bring dance to a
point where it is antithetical to the very idea of the work of art.

In this context, then, and in opposition to Banes's reading, one might
understand historical modern dance to be properly modernist in so far
as, in the name of such a self-determination, it is shaped by an attempt
to overcome its own contingent nature as a *performance*. In this way, the
definition by modern theorists and practitioners alike of dance as an art
whose elements are, as Langer emphasises, 'made' rather than 'found',

which are 'composed' rather than 'framed', and whose significances
inhere within a fixed and unified form, describes the 'art dance' as that
which would overcome its ephemerality as theatre. In *Modern Dance
Forms* Horst emphasises that 'it should never be forgotten that there
must be a form into which the qualities and style can be arranged if the
dance is to have choreographic validity'.[63] Similarly, he calls on Langer
for authority, who states simply that 'Nothing has an aesthetic existence
without form. No dance can be called a work of art unless it has been
deliberately planned and can be repeated.'[64] Such statements flatly suppose that as a performance aspires to the condition of art, so it attempts
to defeat its own ephemeral and contingent nature and acquire the condition of an object.

Consistently with this, and after Fried, one can readily argue that,
however much it strives toward the ideal, no *performance* can be modernist after the manner of Greenberg's project. Such a conclusion does
not attempt to resolve the question of whether modern or postmodern
dance is modernist, but rather looks toward the way in which assumptions inherent within Greenberg's notion of the modernist work begin to
unravel once they are brought into the realm of performance. In turn,
this unravelling sets the ground for a reading of historical postmodern
dance not simply in the terms of a rejection of modern dance styles, but
as a questioning of the assumptions which animate this whole idea of
the modernist project. Far from rehearsing Greenberg's programme
through dance, the historical postmodern dance's reduction of dance to
simply 'movement', or even the presence of the dancer alone, attacks
the very notion of the autonomous work of art, revealing a contingency,
and so an instability, in place of the centre the modernist project would
seek to realise.

Chapter 5

The Collapse of Hierarchies and a Postmodern Dance

The character and development of the early Judson Dance Theater reflected, first of all, the nature of Robert Dunn's classes in choreography from which the Judson group emerged. Held initially in the autumn of 1960 and culminating in the earliest of the dance concerts at the Judson Memorial Church in Greenwich Village in 1962, Dunn began his classes at the Merce Cunningham studio at the invitation of John Cage.[1] Cage himself, following the start of his series of influential courses on 'Composition in Experimental Music' at the New School of 1956–60 which were attended by Allan Kaprow and George Brecht among other artists engaged with Happenings, Fluxus and the new dance, had taught an analogous course on modern dance composition at the request of members of the Cunningham company.[2] Although he was neither a dancer nor a choreographer, Dunn had studied music and dance before attending Cage's classes at the New School and shared both Cage's eclectic interests and his enthusiasm for chance procedures. In his own teaching, Dunn not only drew upon his experience of Cage as a teacher, but sought to make clear methods and principles of composition close to Cage's own. In her detailed account of the history of the Judson Dance Theater, Sally Banes emphasises the variety of influences acting upon Dunn's work and sensibility which, quite apart from his enthusiasm for the contemporary arts, ranged from the Bauhaus to Heidegger, Sartre and Taoism. Nevertheless, Banes concludes, 'for all the diversity of models, the unifying and paradigmatic form of choreography in Dunn's class was the aleatory process.'[3]

The nature and extent of this concern for chance procedure and its implications are evident in the composition of the first of the Judson Dance Theater concerts. Comprised primarily of pieces developed within the composition class, *A Concert of Dance*, presented on 6 July 1962, included work by Judith and Robert Dunn, Bill Davis, Ruth Emerson, Deborah Hay, Fred Herko, David Gordon, Steve Paxton, Yvonne Rainer and Elaine Summers. In their publicity, the group stressed the importance of choreographic process, suggesting that the work would include such means as 'indeterminacy, rules specifying situations, improvisations, spontaneous determination'.[4] While these approaches directly echoed Cage's methods, the pattern of the concert itself introduced another element of chance and drew further on Cage's aesthetic.

Organised so that the identity of individual choreographies might become confused, the programme to *A Concert of Dance* lists 15 items incorporating a total of 23 originally discrete presentations. In this way, dances were presented simultaneously or were at times allowed to run on from one to the next without clear demarcation. In the same spirit, the framing of the concert served to confuse conventional categories. 'Dance number one' was a film, *Overture*, compiled from chance edited footage shot by Elaine Summers and John Herbert McDowell and played as the audience entered the space. The interval, itself listed as the eighth item on the programme, included a performance of Rainer's *Divertissement*, while the concert as a whole ended in darkness as the dancing continued. For *Rafladan*, in which Deborah Hay danced while Alex Hay manipulated a light and Charles Rotmil played a Japanese flute, Banes notes:

> the dancing happened in the dark, suggesting that the movements of a person not directly visible might still fall within the realm of dance. One could see Alex Hay's movements indirectly by watching the lights as he manipulated them. But Deborah Hay's movements were present only by implication.[5]

Within this framework, dances utilising chance procedures were combined with work embracing a variety of styles and methods. While Fred Herko chose to perform a 'barefoot Suzi-Q'[6] to music by Erik Satie in *Once or Twice a Week I Put on Sneakers to Go Uptown*, Ruth Emerson's solo *Timepiece* was created by applying chance procedures to a gamut of predetermined actions, movement qualities, timings and positionings in space. In contrast, David Gordon's *Helen's Dance* had been devised as a rejection of a rigid adherence to chance method and an attempt to circumvent an exercise from one of Dunn's classes, while Rainer's *Divertissement*, Banes recounts, satirised partnered dances in a spoof of the traditional ballet entr'acte of European opera. In other work, chance procedure was combined with alternative means. In *Narrative*, Emerson introduced an element of indeterminacy into performance, giving each of her dancers a score of actions including movements triggered by the activities of other performers. In *The Daily Wake*, Elaine Summers based her selection of movement elements on the photographs and text of newspapers, while the layout of individual pages provided a floorplan for the dance. In yet other pieces connections with Cage were clearly stated. Item number twelve consisted of dances by Ruth Emerson and Carol Scothorn devised by cutting up and reassembling Labanotation and performed as Cage's *Cartridge Music* was played. Extending these kinds of concerns, Summers's *Instant Chance* introduced chance processes into performance. Here individual dancers determined the type, speed and rhythm of their successive movements within parameters defined by repeatedly throwing large styrofoam blocks as if they were giant dice. For Summers the piece evidenced the process of its own making while engendering a spontaneity and sense of play.

For Yvonne Rainer and Steve Paxton, as for many of the others, chance procedure provided an important method amongst a variety of means. While in *Ordinary Dance*, Rainer combined her own choice and organisation of movement with autobiographic text, in *Dance for 3 People and 6 Arms* she allowed her performers free and improvised choices from a gamut of previously determined movements. Punctuated by certain actions which would trigger a given sequence for all three performers, the 15-minute piece looked towards the dancers' remaking of Rainer's choreography through its very complexity, which itself introduced an indeterminacy into performance. Similarly, while in *Transit* Paxton 'presented a spectrum of movement styles, from classical dance (ballet) to "marked dance" ... to pedestrian movement' in a procedure he describes as 'just taking items and playing their scales',[7] in *Proxy* he sought to give up aspects of his own authority as choreographer. In response to work with Cage's scores, Paxton sought to use chance procedure to select as well as organise movement. Rather than communicating his movement choices directly, Paxton employed a photo-score made up from sports photographs to mediate between choreography and performer. While he was involved in a selection process, decisions affecting fundamental aspects of the presentation were left open to each participant. In this way:

I made the score and handed it over to the performers, and they could take a linear or circular path through the score. You could start any place you wanted to, but then you went all the way through it. You did as many repeats as were indicated. But how long it took and what you did between postures was not set at all.[8]

As these various departures suggest, Cage's practice provides a point from which the early Judson presentations at once drew and against which they defined themselves. Such an equivocal relationship with Cage's means and purposes make his work an important point of reference from which to consider the underlying logic of these strategies.

Chance method and the object of art

Through the concert-hall performance of the first of his 'silent pieces' in 1952, Cage sought to clarify the principles underlying his work as a whole. In his closing of the piano lid for the duration of each of its three movements, David Tudor's original presentation of *4'33"* made absolutely clear Cage's denial of conventional musical vocabularies. In pointedly refusing to fill the 'silence' of what was evidently presented as a musical piece while insisting on a playing out of three timed movements, Cage sought to invite an attention to the 'noise' of the environment, to whatever sounds happened to fall within a durational frame. For Cage, the piece, which he had conceived of as early as 1941,[9] made clear the discovery in which his work was rooted, that:

nothing takes place but sounds: those that are notated and those that are not. Those that are not notated appear in the written music as silences, opening the doors of the music to the sounds that happen to be in the environment ... There is no such thing as an empty space or an empty time. There is always something to see, something to hear .... [10]

Such a conception of 'music' explicitly attacks the notion of the autonomy of the work of art; its separation of itself from its mundane environment. In its performance, *4'33"* strips the musical work of everything but a context and the listener's experience of her own presence. In doing so, the piece explicitly rejects the notion of the self-contained, self-sustaining 'object' and redraws the work of art as an occasion or event marked out by a self-reflexive attention or receptivity. In Cage's own terms *4'33"* offers each viewer 'a discipline which, accepted, in

4' 33"

FOR ANY INSTRUMENT OR COMBINATION OF INSTRUMENTS

John Cage

NOTE: THE TITLE OF THIS WORK IS THE TOTAL LENGTH IN MINUTES AND
SECONDS OF ITS PERFORMANCE. AT WOODSTOCK, N.Y., AUGUST 29. 1952,
THE TITLE WAS 4'33" AND THE THREE PARTS WERE 33", 2'40", AND
1'20". IT WAS PERFORMED BY DAVID TUDOR, PIANIST, WHO INDI-
CATED THE BEGINNINGS OF PARTS BY CLOSING, THE ENDINGS BY OPEN-
ING, THE KEYBOARD LID. AFTER THE WOODSTOCK PERFORMANCE, A
COPY IN PROPORTIONAL NOTATION WAS MADE FOR IRWIN KREMEN.
IN IT THE TIMELENGTHS OF THE MOVEMENTS WERE 30", 2'23", AND 1'
40". HOWEVER, THE WORK MAY BE PERFORMED BY ANY INSTRUMEN-
TALIST(S) AND THE MOVEMENTS MAY LAST ANY LENGTHS OF TIME.

FOR IRWIN KREMEN

© 1960 by Henmar Press Inc., 373 Park Ave. S., New York, NY 10016; reproduced by kind
permission of Peters Edition Ltd, London.

I

TACET

II

TACET

III

TACET

0'00"
SOLO TO BE PERFORMED IN ANY WAY BY ANYONE

FOR YOKO ONO AND TOSHI ICHIYANAGI
TOKYO , OCT. 24 , 1962
John Cage

IN A SITUATION PROVIDED WITH MAXIMUM AMPLIFICATION (NO FEEDBACK), PERFORM
A DISCIPLINED ACTION.

WITH ANY INTERRUPTIONS.
FULFILLING IN WHOLE OR PART AN OBLIGATION TO OTHERS.
NO TWO PERFORMANCES TO BE OF THE SAME ACTION, NOR MAY THAT ACTION BE
THE PERFORMANCE OF A 'MUSICAL' COMPOSITION.
NO ATTENTION TO BE GIVEN THE SITUATION (ELECTRONIC, MUSICAL, THEATRICAL).
10·25·62

THE FIRST PERFORMANCE WAS THE WRITING OF THIS MANUSCRIPT (FIRST MARGINATION ONLY).

THIS IS 4'33" (NO.2) AND ALSO PT.3 OF A WORK OF WHICH ATLAS ECLIPTICALIS IS PT.1.

© 1962 by Henmar Press Inc., 373 Park Ave. S., New York, NY 10016; reproduced by
kind permission of Peters Edition Ltd, London.

turn accepts whatever',[11] and looks toward a mode of attention, a 'performance' to be made by the listener, and one which could be realised quite independently of any concert-hall presentation such as Tudor's. Cage suggests:

> What really pleases me in that silent piece is that it can be played at any time, but it only comes alive when you play it. And each time you do, it is an experience of being very, very much alive.[12]

In his revision of *4'33"*, *0'00"(4'33" No. 2)* (1962), 'a solo to be performed in any way by anyone', Cage sought to clarify the implications of this invitation. Read as a description of an active looking and against the terms of *4'33"*, the frame Cage describes here is not dependent upon a given duration but a 'disciplined action' taken up by the viewer, in which a heightened attention ('maximum amplification') is exercised and 'all interruptions' accepted. Whereas *4'33"* is 'musical', *0'00"* accepts no such limitation, and while *4'33"* can be associated with a particular formal circumstance, here Cage bars any such simple definition. In this way, Cage defines a work which comes into being through the spectator's actions alone, which literally consists of and is defined by a committed self-reflexive attention.

Plainly, Cage's understanding of the terms by which such a 'work of art' is defined opposes any notion of the work's separation of itself from its context and the differentiation of one 'art-gender' from another. Where the identity of the 'work' is dependent upon only a mode of attention, then not only can the work of art have no independent existence but, by implication, the formal characteristics of the visual and performing arts converge, finding their common ground in the occasion of theatre, the event of their definition by the viewer. In this context, too, it becomes clear that for Cage the notion of the 'object' in which meaning inheres is a construction of the conventional and exclusive hierarchies that define the inherited languages of art. In playing upon the viewer's desire to perceive the elements of a work in a given, stable and so safe relationship, Cage argues, these hierarchies effect a distortion of an otherwise perfectly tangible reality:

> You say: the real, the world as it. But it is not, it becomes! It doesn't wait for us to change ... It is more mobile than you can imagine. You are getting closer to reality when you say that it 'presents itself'; that means it is not there, existing as an object. The world, the real, is not an object. It is a process.[13]

In this sense, conventional musical compositions deny their audience access to the actual nature of the sounds of which they are made up, rehearsing, instead, an understanding of the work and so the world as 'object'. Cage notes:

> When you listen to sounds that share a periodic rhythm, what you hear is necessarily something other than the sounds themselves. You don't hear the sounds – you hear the fact they're organized.[14]

It follows that for Cage, where 'art should introduce us to life'[15] as a process, a resistance to the presence of the object in art is fundamental to the value of the work. Such a resistance does not simply mean the pursuit of an ephemerality or the privileging of one kind of predetermination over another. Instead, it involves an undermining or disruption of the 'perceived' object and so an uncovering of the work's inherent instability; its dependency upon the attitude and intention of the viewer, the fact that 'through the way I place my intention, I create the experience that I have'.[16] Through his use of chance method in the process of composition and development of indeterminacy in performance itself, Cage sought to cast off conventional values and hierarchies and with them the ways of looking these conventions invite and imply. Thus, he tells us, through his early use of chance procedures drawn from the *I Ching*, he wished to come to 'a musical composition the continuity of which is free of individual taste and memory (psychology) and also of the literature and tradition of art'.[17]

Between chance and the personal image

The relationship between Cage's work and the various departures of the Judson Dance Theater is a complex one. In the first place, in utilising chance method for the selection as well as organisation of movement, the Judson dancers replay Cage's overturning of hierarchies. Most immediately, then, the distinctions upon which the conventional vocabularies of dance are based, classical or modern, are thrown into confusion. More particularly, where chance is used to determine the nature and selection of elements, the choreographer moves to collapse the conventional distinctions between that which is and is not 'proper' to the 'art dance'. Such consequences are apparent within *A Concert of Dance*. As a result of the chance procedures used in the composition of *Timepiece*, which was unaccompanied, Emerson recalls that 'to my utter horror ... I had to get over the fact that I could start the piece with forty seconds of stillness. One of the reasons that I liked the piece was that I learned I could do that.'[18] Where Elaine Summers introduced chance procedure into performance through the game structure of *Instant Chance*, similar 'natural rhythms' entered into the work. Thus, Banes observes, rather than seek to sustain a sense of 'performance', of presentation, the performers of *Instant Chance* were forced to concentrate 'on doing the task at hand – over and over', continually abandoning 'one movement for no obvious reason to throw their "dice" for the next instruction'.[19] Just as these transitions arise from the focus of the performers upon the playing of a game rather than the presentation of specific movement qualities, so the rules of the game themselves provide for a disruption of the 'performed' tasks. Again, Banes recounts:

> Though each performer is highly self-absorbed, there is some interaction. The instructions for this performance ... often had one dancer lifting his colleagues one at a time, or interrupting, or in other ways intervening in their movements ... The effect was that of a bratty child bothering his playmates.[20]

Instant Chance offers itself up as a game through which unpredictable actions and movements are found. In this way Summers pursues not only an indeterminacy with regard to the organisation of movement choices but, in certain respects, a giving up of her own control in order that apparently 'untransformed' elements may be offered to the viewer. Similarly, for Steve Paxton, such strategies complimented and extended his giving up of his own authority as choreographer. In *Proxy*, while his use of the photo-score served to disrupt the usual relationship between choreography and performance, his choice of movement also introduced an indeterminacy into the process of composition by calling on the idiosyncratic movements of his participants. Banes notes that the dance involved not only 'standing in a basin full of ball-bearings; getting into poses taken from photographs; drinking a glass of water; and eating a pear' but also 'a great deal of walking'.[21] Here the very ordinariness of movement such as eating or walking allows a giving up of specific controls. Paxton suggests:

> Walking is something you can't tamper with. If you say 'ordinary walking,' you get a wide range of materials. And the more you tamper with it, the less it has the quality of being just the thing. It starts to look like somebody with a problem on their mind or somebody with

an infirmity instead of just someone walking. I tried not to tamper with it too much, so that it wasn't too special and it just occurred.[22]

The association of chance method with such a breakdown of distinctions is evident in the earliest of the Judson explorations. In the first of Dunn's series of classes with just five participants, Paulus Berenson, Marni Mahaffay, Simone Forti, Steve Paxton and Yvonne Rainer,[23] a use of chance method served to confuse the notion of what was admissible and inadmissible as part of a dance presentation. For Mahaffay, Banes suggests, the classes offered an understanding of Cage's notion of silence, and, by implication, the idea that 'any movement is valid as a part of dance – "whether it's a cough, a sniffle, or natural movement"'.[24] Similarly, Paxton presented work consisting simply of removing furniture from an office at speed or 'sitting on a bench, eating a sandwich'.[25] Simone Forti's *See-Saw* and *Rollers*, which were performed as part of a programme of 'new happenings' at the Reuben Gallery in December 1960 in collaboration with Robert Morris and other artists, drew on children's activities and games to an analogous end. Seeing her own choices as a matter of placing 'an effective act within the interplay of many forces',[26] Forti used a see-saw and roller carts to place her performers in precarious relationships which threatened a loss of control, so focusing the participants' improvisations and introducing unpredictable qualities which would 'automatically become an element in their performance'.[27] In such work as this, Morris observes, the very complexity and difficulty of rules and relationships 'effectively blocked the dancer's performing "set" and reduced him to frantically attempting to respond to events – reduced him from performance to action'.[28]

In this work, then, where 'any movement is valid as a part of dance', the notion that the identity and meaning of a work is a matter of the formal properties it possesses, that there must be something 'within' a dance that separates it out from its mundane context, falls away. Rather than pursue a self-critical honing of dance toward the essence of the medium, a casting away of the 'unessential', these presentations throw out the attempt to differentiate between that which is and is not proper and necessary to dance. Such consequences are evident not only through the presentation of 'found' movement and everyday tasks, as well as the free combination of a wide range of departures and styles which characterised the Judson concerts, but also in direct challenges to the conventional distinctions between artistic media. So Trisha Brown, among others, was concerned to address 'dance' problems through a self-conscious exchange with other disciplines. In responding to Dunn's assignment to make a three-minute dance, she recalls:

> Dick Levine taught himself to cry and did so for the full period while I held a stopwatch instructed by him to shout just before the time elapsed, 'Stop it! Stop it! Cut it out!' both of us ending at exactly three minutes. That dance is a good example of the practice of substituting one medium, in this case acting/crying, to solve a dance problem.[29]

Here too, though, it is also important to set the role of chance method into context. Despite the importance of a use of chance to an overthrowing of prevailing assumptions and practice, aleatory processes clearly do not, in themselves, underpin and shape these various strategies. It is at this point, then, that significant differences between the Judson presentations and Cage's own work become evident.

As is clear from his silent pieces, where in Cage's work art seeks to 'introduce us to life', it does so by offering a discipline through which composer, performer and viewer may resist, in certain respects, their own imposition upon the materials they meet. For Cage, these notions are informed by an involvement with Zen Bhuddism. As a consequence of his studies with the Zen teacher D. T. Suzuki between 1946 and 1950, Cage came to shape his work through disciplines appropriate to the Zen pursuit of 'no-mind'. Distinguishing between *M*ind, or that which is beyond the intentions and will of the individual, and *m*ind, or the ego, Cage remarks:

> If one is involved just with Mind, and not with the arts, one sits cross-legged in order to come to no-mind. But if you're already, as I was, involved with music, then you have to control your likes and dislikes with something as strict as sitting cross-legged. So I used chance operations.[30]

While Cage's uses of aleatory processes are shaped by the nature and purposes of this discipline, for most of the choreographers associated with the Judson Dance Theater, as for many other artists drawing on Cage's work, chance method evidently effects a release from conventional hierarchies and introduces new concerns without establishing itself as a single means or set of parameters. The significance of this becomes quite apparent in that work which follows *A Concert of Dance*. While a second concert was constituted largely of work from the first presentation at the Judson Church, concerts three and four of January

1963 consisted of performances developed by the group following the end of Dunn's classes in the previous autumn. Stressing the pluralism of the group's work, the concerts introduced presentations which, in general, moved away from chance method and yet continued to be concerned in part with elements and patterns chance processes had offered an address to. These performances called on the work of untrained performers and everyday movements such as running and walking, as well as such compositional means as juxtaposition, repetition and structured improvisation, while incorporating monologues, tasks, the use of objects and even romantic music.[31]

In this way, even these early concerts marked not only a departure from the direct influence of Cage's methods but also from Dunn, whose approaches and aims coincided closely with Cage's. In a lecture written as early as 1961 or 1962, Yvonne Rainer gave voice to this difference, describing various meetings in her work between the chance operation and the 'image', the 'personal vision, fantasy, or dream and attendant atmosphere'. In doing so, she proposed a meeting between chance method and precisely the play of personal taste and intention Cage's disciplines were dedicated to overcoming. Rainer suggests:

There is no innate contradiction between the chance operation and the image.

Aside from the image possibilities in the use of chance – and by this I mean the assimilation of the results of a chance operation into one's own personal language and imagery – all this aside – it is possible for the chance result and the image to co-exist.

It is possible for the image to influence one's interpretation of the chance operation.

It is also possible for the image to be so strong and insistent that it makes other kinds of investigation unnecessary.

It is also possible – and very gratifying when it happens to me – for the chance operation to control certain aspects of a larger image. But here again is a situation where the image – also the experience and life of the artist – has been affected by the use of chance.[32]

Rainer's lecture clearly draws upon a sensibility that can be related to Cage's work, reflecting not only a concern to open the work to elements and influences beyond the author's control but also for the significance of chance to wider choices and experiences. At the same time, though, Rainer sees no conflict between the exercise of personal taste and the use of aleatory processes and is concerned for the variety of relationships that may exist between the two. Evidently, too, this openness was not simply a matter of Rainer's particular approach, but was an important aspect of the concerts themselves. In her review of concerts three and four, Jill Johnston concluded:

> The possibilities of form and movement have become unlimited. There is no way to make a dance; there is no kind of movement that can't be included in these dances; there is no kind of sound that is not proper for accompaniment.[33]

This very openness begs the question of precisely what notion of dance the Judson work marks out. Here, clearly, while aleatory processes have been instrumental in effecting a collapse of the oppositions upon which the notion of the self-contained and autonomous work depends, chance operations have not in themselves taken the place of this hierarchy as the means by which the work is defined. Indeed, it would seem that this work does not project itself toward the inherent and unique significance of dance-movement or attempt, after Cage, to produce its antithesis, a 'work' which, free of 'intention' and 'purpose', reaches toward another 'truth', to something quite beyond the claim to hierarchy or meaning.

Being seen: minimalism and process

Yvonne Rainer describes her *Trio A* of 1966 in terms analogous to those of minimal art. In her essay 'A Quasi Survey of Some "Minimalist" Tendencies in the Quantitatively Minimal Dance Activity Midst the Plethora, or an Analysis of *Trio A*' of the same year, Rainer emphasised her rejection of both formal and thematic development:

> Variation was not a method of development. No one of the individual movements in the series was made by varying a quality in any other...In the strict sense neither is there any repetition.[34]

In this context, and rather than emerge out of a focus upon the generation of movement-elements through tasks, actions in relation to objects, or rulegames, Rainer suggests, *Trio A*, which is comprised of many simple task-like actions performed in the mid-range of bodily extension, is constituted first of all through an attention to the 'look' of the performance as it unfolds before an audience. While the piece is constructed without variation of any of its elements, in its performance, Rainer notes, she allows no pauses between phrases, ensuring that 'each phrase merges immediately into the next with no observable accent'.[35] While a great variety of shapes occur, in their continuity, she suggests, 'no one part of the series is made any more important than any other'[36] as each is given an equal weight and so an equal emphasis. Here, and while Rainer averts her gaze from the audience in order that the sequence may seem 'worklike rather than exhibitionlike', the phrasing of both movement-elements and transitions serve to ensure:

> What is seen is a control that seems geared to the *actual* time it takes the *actual* weight of the body to go through the prescribed motions, rather than an adherence to an imposed ordering of time. In other words, the demands made on the body's (actual) energy resources appear to be commensurate with the task – be it getting up from the floor, raising an arm, tilting the pelvis, etc. – much as one would get up out of a chair, reach for a high shelf, or walk downstairs when one is not in a hurry.[37]

After Cage, such a presentation can be read as a deliberate frustration of the viewer's attempt to understand one element in terms of another. In her analysis of the piece, Rainer remarks that 'my *Trio A* dealt with the "seeing" difficulty by dint of its continual and unremitting revelation of gestural detail that did *not* repeat itself, thereby focusing on the fact that the material could not easily be encompassed'.[38] By its very complexity, *Trio A* resists the attempt to 'contain' it; to read it, predict it, to set its boundaries. It follows that the very 'difficulty' of reading the dance looks toward a disruption or a staving off of the 'object', the construction of a developing 'whole'.

While doing this, and in opposition to Cage's work, however, *Trio A* explicitly incorporates both classical and modern figures. Susan Foster notes that *Trio A* makes specific reference to 'the conventional lines of design-oriented dance' and offers 'fleeting glimpses of classical placement',[39] while Rainer's 'sustained, smooth transfer of weight' is, she suggests, 'reminiscent of the organic successivity of expressionist movement'.[40] Here, then, *Trio A* subjects quotations of familiar line and figure to this 'minimalism', treating conventional phrases as 'tasks' whose actual effort is to be exposed. In doing so, Sally Banes suggests, *Trio A* comes to operate 'dialectically', bringing 'classical lines and gesture into conflict with their own subversions'.[41] Rainer herself points to the 'reversal of a kind of illusionism'[42] out of which *Trio A* is constituted and acknowledges that her incorporation of conventional elements involves an inversion of the styles of performance they recall. In achieving the 'look' of *Trio A*, Rainer notes:

> one must bring to bear many different degrees of effort just in getting from one thing to another ... The irony here is ... [that] I have exposed a type of effort where it has been traditionally concealed and have concealed phrasing where it has been traditionally displayed.[43]

Such means qualify and extend Rainer's negotiation with the viewer. In exposing the actual effort of conventional phrases while placing them amongst simple task-like activities, Rainer specifically attacks the conventional distinctions between the 'natural rhythms' of functional movement and the 'transformed' or 'heightened' nature of 'dance-movement'. Yet such a treatment of quotation clearly goes further than an attack upon hierarchical vocabularies. In explicitly denying conventional phrases the disguise and elaboration upon which their usual significances depend, *Trio A* throws its own task-based mode of execution into relief. Through its play with expectation, its *denial* of conventional weight and significance to that which it appropriates, *Trio A* at once presents a critique of the nature and effect of conventional stylisation while exposing its own particular construction of movement-elements, its own 'minimalist style'. It follows that, here, the critique of style, of the 'giving' of meaning to movement-elements, extends to *Trio A*'s own means, as the series of denials it constitutes itself through are revealed as yet another manipulation and play with movement. In this way *Trio A* engages overtly with possible readings of movement, catching its elements between those 'styles' and so significances they recall and their construction as 'tasks' through a self-consciously minimalist mode of execution. Such a play with the 'reading' of movement is far from a revelation of that which is inherently 'significant' or legitimate within dance, but is an exposure of the dependency of movement for its character upon a negotiation between dancer and observer, upon an address to the nature and fact of its being read.

In contrast to Rainer's complex montages, Steve Paxton's concern with walking, which was established as early as 1962 in such pieces as *Proxy* and *Transit*, pursue a different kind of 'minimalism', not only through a giving up of the choreographer's authority but through a simplification of both the work and its elements. In *State* (1968), 42 performers presented themselves to an audience in 'a random, scattered group' and simply stood for two three-minute intervals, while in *Smiling* (1969) two performers smiled for five minutes.[44] For Banes, though, it is in *Satisfyin Lover* (1967) that Paxton presents the apotheosis of walking. Here, between 30 and 84 performers, divided into six groups, walk across an imaginary track ten feet wide, stretching from entrance to exit in a space, which, in its first performance, was 200 feet long. Three chairs, set in the centre of this area and slightly forward of the track, provide for an interruption of the walking as performers sit, stand and then return to their crossing of the space. While Paxton's score offers simply cues for activities, number of steps and the timing of pauses, his notes to performers emphasise the informal and individual nature of their actions:

> The pace is an easy walk, but not slow. Performance manner is serene and collected.
> The dance is about walking, standing, and sitting. Try to keep these elements clear and pure.
> The gaze is to be directed forward relative to the body, but should not be especially fixed. The mind should be at rest.[45]

Rather than transform individual movement-elements or establish qualities and patterns that might suggest a self-contained and articulate 'dance', Paxton facilitates an exhibition of walking, sitting and standing in the simplest possible way. Paxton's choices would seem to have been made precisely in order that the elements of *Satisfyin Lover* should remain not only unpredictable but, in their unself-conscious variety, acquire no significance, value or quality which could immediately distinguish them from the viewer's own act of walking or even presence in the space. It follows that the identity of such an activity as 'dance' becomes openly dependent upon the occasion of theatre. Reviewing a later presentation of *Satisfyin Lover*, the critic Jill Johnston focuses precisely upon this fact, attending to the very ordinary and apparently untransformed nature of movement-activity and its blurring of the distinction between 'movement' and 'dance-movement'. She draws attention to:

> the incredible assortment of bodies ... walking one after the other across the gymnasium in their any old clothes. The fat, the skinny, the

medium, the slouched and slumped, the straight and tall, the bow-legged and knock-kneed, the awkward, the elegant, the coarse, the delicate, the pregnant, the virginal, the you name it, by implication every postural possibility in the postural spectrum, that's you and me in all our ordinary everyday who cares postural splendour.[46]

Through its very simplicity, *Satisfyin Lover* makes visible the contingent nature of its identity as 'dance'. Rather than look inward, towards a legitimating core or interior quality, *Satisfyin Lover* looks outward, towards the viewer and her 'framing' of these activities as a dance.

On the basis of *Trio A* and *Satisfyin Lover*, one might readily read the 'pared-down' or 'minimal' dance of the Judson concerts as a resistance to those inherited languages which would stabilise the work, which would 'give' it meaning, in favour of a play of instability and contingency that might provoke an awareness of a dance's definition through the way in which it is seen. Indeed, what becomes evident through such a reading is the variety of means dedicated to such a self-reflexive negotiation with the observer.

Although usually associated with the 'cool' or 'analytical' aspects of the Judson performances, the work of Lucinda Childs, like that of Rainer herself, is characterised by a wide variety of means and a development through apparently radical change. In her own consideration of her work, though, Childs has emphasised a continuity which she describes first of all in terms of an attention to the viewer. Originally inspired by Cunningham and influenced by Cage and the choreographies of Robert Morris, Steve Paxton and Yvonne Rainer, Childs's early approaches were rooted in combining dance phrases with movement-activity in relation to objects and, later, in the juxtaposition of movement and language. In this context, and like Rainer, Childs sought to escape 'traditional dance vocabulary' through task-activity 'governed by the materials and subject to the limitations of their physical qualities'.[47] At the same time, though, Childs's monologues serve to set movement which might escape any conventional notion of choreographic pattern against a clear and obviously imposed structure. Childs notes:

The dialogues did not in and of themselves dictate action, but accompanied action as the activity in the dance drifted in and out of a context that was relevant to the content of the dialogue. And I determined the extent to which relevance between action and dialogue was sustained intermittently throughout the individual dances.[48]

In a piece such as *Street Dance* of July 1964 the disjunctive relationship between movement-activity and imposed structure is extended to the point where the audience's ability to 'see' the performance at all becomes dependent upon the monologue that frames it. Here, while the audience watches from a loft across the street, two performers engage in a six-minute sequence of activities entirely based on their 'found surroundings' and which are 'blended in with the other activity ... going on in the street'.[49] As Childs's taped voice describes the street in detail, the dancers engage in activities largely indistinguishable from the general activity around them, and punctuate their actions regularly, though momentarily, by pointing out that to which Childs's monologue refers. In this way, because at such a distance the viewer is unable to see the detail of that which the dancers point towards, Childs notes:

> the spectator was called upon to envision, in an imagined sort of way, information that in fact existed beyond the range of actual perception, so that a kind of cross-reference of perception tended to take place in which one mode of perceiving had to reconcile itself with the other to rule out the built-in discrepancy that the situation created.[50]

Street Dance plays on the discrepancy between that which the observer's attention is drawn towards and that which she can readily perceive, so provoking an awareness of looking. In doing so, though, *Street Dance* puts its own terms and parameters into question. Faced with a performance that is repeatedly lost to the unself-conscious activities of non-performers, and which is dependent for its distinction from the 'everyday' on a monologue which describes a place rather than an activity, these strategies would seem to put the very possibility of the definition of a 'work' into question. The purpose of the taped monologue is not so much to 'reveal' a dance as to put the observer into the position of defining the 'work', of negotiating between elements and means that have an ambivalent relationship to one another in a piece whose identity as a 'dance', let alone its particular parameters, are uncertain. Here, then, and in other such pieces where apparently 'everyday' or 'ordinary' movement-activities are set against a self-conscious frame, the observer is drawn toward an awareness of her own pivotal position in the definition of the piece.

Such a drawing of the viewer into a self-conscious process of definition underpins a range of strategies shaping Childs's work and is apparent from its inception. In *Geranium* of February 1965, a dance of four sections, Childs used the third section to announce the fact that there was no third section and offered instead 'theoretical reasons for dealing with the gap'.[51] In *Model* of August 1964, Childs's movement was accompanied by her description of a 'typical modern dance position':

It is uncomfortable to be in as well as difficult to get out of and ugly.
The right foot is bent diagonally back toward the right and the left leg is bent diagonally back toward the left.
It is an expressive position.
Expressive for someone who has nothing to do.[52]

These commentaries play with the possible significance of structure, movement and dialogue, yet remain disarmingly self-reflexive. Here, while the significance of the lack of a third section becomes the substance of the third section, the 'typical modern dance position' is drained of its would-be 'expressivity' by Childs's description of the relationship between mechanics and purpose as well as the fact of the narrative itself. Such devices echo the quotations of *Trio A*, where the familiar phrase or line is denied its usual place and import, and is incorporated or appropriated in order that it may be subverted, put into question.

Formally, though, it is Childs's later work which converges with Rainer's. Beginning with *Untitled Trio* of 1968, Childs became concerned to apply a set of elements to a dance as variables, allowing identical phrase sequences to be repeated while being subject to 'reversals, subdivisions, inversions, reordering in space, and displacement from one dancer to another'.[53] In this way, and with seating on all sides in order to establish as many points of view as possible, Childs sought to create a situation in which 'the same thing is seen again and again but never in exactly the same way'.[54] In her solo *Particular Reel* (1973), Childs traversed 21 parallel lines, performing a three-minute phrase that covered one-third of the space, repeating it in reverse for the second third, and again in the original manner for the final third. Despite the apparent simplicity of the system the relationship between movement-activity and its organisation was such that the viewer was faced with a continually changing sequence. In *Particular Reel*, while a series of reversals allowed ends to link with ends and beginnings with beginnings, in the manner of 1234567654321234567, Childs's choice of movements for her original phrase served to introduce a complexity into this apparently simple structure, as the elements of the phrase mirrored and reversed one another. Childs notes:

While the dancer is fully cognizant of the particular adjustment she is abiding by, the spectator is not. He is introduced to the phenomena gradually during the passage of time, and the structure becomes apparent to him as configurations perceived outside the moment are matched up with those seen in the moment. While any configuration tends to dissolve in the memory as others replace it, the deliberate simplicity of the action tends to counteract that process. The perceptual bind that the viewer is drawn into, nevertheless, is reminiscent of the same kind of double focus provoked by the earlier pieces. Either he perceives that the same thing is different when it is not, or he perceives the same thing as the same through an awareness of the manner in which it has been removed from its original mode of presentation. In drifting between prediction and speculation, he is dislodged from any single point of view.[55]

Working its way through Childs's various kinds of presentations is a pursuit of a self-reflexive address to the process of looking. It is through such a focus that Childs's and Rainer's work may be seen as closely related despite their formal differences. *Particular Reel* operates by way of variation and elaboration, and so by those 'developments' *Trio A* rejects. Nevertheless, in so far as Childs's variations continually draw the spectator into readings from which she is dislodged, forcing a self-consciousness on behalf of the viewer as she views, these patterns serve an analogous function to Rainer's subversions of style.

In this context, aspects of Trisha Brown's later work can be read as exemplifying both the 'reductive' performance associated with the Judson presentations and a self-reflexive attention to the process of being seen. Rooted in her work with Ann Halprin on task-based choreography and, shortly afterwards, in her experimentation with chance and other methods in Dunn's classes, Brown's work has taken many departures and yet has tended to centre around the notion of 'improvisation within set boundaries'.[56] As her work has developed it has been upon the importance of these boundaries rather than particular movement choices, that her concerns have focused. In her 'Equipment Dances' of the late 1960s and early 1970s, such as *Man Walking Down the Side of a Building* (1969), Brown sought situations where the 'boundaries' of the piece, including its very difficulty, precluded movement choice. Here, where a dancer is equipped to walk down a seven-storey building:

Aside from the equipment and danger the piece was very direct. I knew when to start – it starts at the top. I knew where the dancer went – he went straight down. ... The movement that he did between top and the bottom was walking. There were so few choices; the structure, the set-up, made the choices. Now *that* comes out of my view on making and choreographing movement ... there are a thousand choices – I mean why is this better than that?[57]

Rather than concern herself with defining a dance through the presentation of particular movement qualities, Brown attends to the relationship between activity and frame and, through this, to the viewer's act of looking. In her review 'Walking on the Wall', Deborah Jowitt recorded her self-conscious vacillation between the 'uncanny' illusion of an everyday activity and the display of skill and equipment the frame itself necessitated:

> For dizzying moments at a time, you seem to be in a tower looking down on the foreshortened bodies of people promenading endlessly on two intersecting white streets. Sometimes you come down from the tower to watch the technique of it all – how they get into and out of the slings, how they pass, how they unstick a recalcitrant pulley, how they zoom around a corner.[58]

In this presentation no particular choice of movement-element is 'better' than any other in the sense that the definition of the piece is not, first of all, dependent upon any such choice. Indeed, in catching the viewer's attention between an acceptance of illusion and an attention to the frame, the Equipment Pieces would force a recognition of the dependence of these elements for what they 'are' on the manner of the viewer's own attention to them.

Consistently with this, and in her own discussion of her 'Accumulation Pieces', dances which in their performance continually evidence an accumulation of actions, Brown has clarified this point. Here, she suggests, while the choreographer is free to be 'seduced' by movement choices, 'the more important issue is how any movement is organized into a dance'.[59] In *Primary Accumulation* of 1972, Brown's dancers engaged in an 18-minute procedure whereby a sequence of 30 actions were accumulated one by one through the continual repetition of an extending string of movements, in the manner of 1; 1,2; 1,2,3; 1,2,3,4. Including movements 'based on formal arrangements of the body parts', 'gestures of universal meanings', 'eccentric actions' and actions with sexual overtones,[60] the procedure sought not only to demonstrate its own framing and reframing of material, but at moments deliberately called this process into question. Actions 3, 4 and 30, Brown notes, are familiar gestures performed in order to raise the question 'is she dancing or has she stopped?'[61] Just as it draws the viewer into a continual re-reading of movement-elements, at several moments *Performance Accumulation* presents activities which put into question whether or not a dance is continuing, yet which, in their repetition, are 'transformed' into dance-movement. In this way *Performance Accumulation* evidences its making as a 'dance', exposing a 'transformation' of 'functional', 'non-dance' activity into 'dance-movement' through a negotiation over framing and so over reading.

Like the Equipment Dances, the Accumulation Pieces suggest that a dance is defined through the way in which it is seen. Again, Brown's comments have reflected this position. In an interview of 1973, and in response to the suggestion that in her accumulation pieces she entered into a process of 'stripping movement to its core', Brown responded by putting the very possibility of such a 'reduction' into question, concluding that 'Most choreographers find a structure and anytime they make a new piece they make a new movement. Whereas I'm using the same movement and making new structures each time. The movement is immaterial.'[62]

If a dance's identity is a matter of circumstances, of 'framing', and so of the way it is seen, then the notion of 'stripping movement to its core' cannot make sense. In this context, neither movement nor dance can be said to have a 'core', for neither is in 'possession' of an identity that can be separated out from the particular meaning or meanings it acquires for those who meet it at the point at which it is met. Indeed, what flows from this position is that, because of the very contingent nature of its meaning and so identity, any element may become a dance or part of a dance by being brought into a negotiation with, or becoming subject to, that 'look', that 'reading', which holds the key to its possible definition.

Being read: Process to narrative

It is in terms of the definition of the dance and its elements through a self-reflexive attention to the process of being seen, that ostensibly 'minimal' performance finds itself on common ground with presentations which overtly incorporate familiar figures and conventions. On this basis, one can trace a consistent development rather than a transformation of means in the work of Yvonne Rainer and, later, Steve Paxton and Trisha Brown, as their work moves away from the overtly 'minimal' and towards an address to conventional dramatic continuities and theatrical forms and devices.

After the final version of *The Mind is a Muscle* in 1968, which had originally incorporated *Trio A* as its first part, Yvonne Rainer's work shifted direction. Following performances in 1968 and 1969 in which she sought to bring aspects of the rehearsal process into the performance itself, Rainer's *Continuous Project – Altered Daily* of 1969 initiated two years of improvisational work with the Grand Union, a collaborative group founded by the performers of the *Project* and which included Steve Paxton and Trisha Brown.

Rainer's dance piece was constructed after Robert Morris's 'process piece' *Continuous Project Altered Daily* of the same year. However, while for Morris the *Project* marked a direct extension of the concerns that had brought him to a 'minimalist' vocabulary, for Rainer the piece led to a departure from the formal conventions and critical vocabulary of minimalism.

In his essay, 'Some Notes on the Phenomenology of Making', Morris emphasised his concern for the process of 'art making', describing an art in which 'process becomes a part of the work instead of prior to it' and where 'forming is moved further into the presentation'.[63] For Morris such concerns stemmed from doubts surrounding the efficacy of the geometrical forms predominant within minimalist work and a desire to develop the logic of the minimalist object even further. Morris's introduction of non-rigid materials into his presentations from 1967 responded directly to the privileging of the cubic and the rectangular in the minimalist practice which he, among others, had defined. In his 'felt pieces', dating from 1967 and 1968, and consisting of sheets, strips or bundles of felt, Morris offered examples of work subject to an open-ended process of change. Shaped and reshaped by the accidents of transportation and exhibition, these objects promise a changing morphology limited only by the particular physical properties of the material itself.

Despite Morris's emphasis upon process, however, and while such 'sculpture' will be changed by the process of being shown, the felt pieces are inevitably presented as product, a particular result of a process now arrested. It is this tension between process and object that Morris's *Continuous Project Altered Daily* dramatises. In the form in which it was presented at the Castelli warehouse in January 1969,[64] the *Project* can be read as being caught between its material elements and the process of change to which they are subject. Installed in a single large room and ostensibly consisting of earth, water, grease, plastic, threads and felt distributed randomly across low wooden tables and the floor of the space, Morris's presentation consisted of the 'alteration' of these materials, first by adding elements and then by removing them.

For the viewer, admitted not to the actual removal of materials but to eight 'stages' of the work, stages documented by an accumulating series of photographs pinned to the wall, the piece sites itself between a process of making or altering and the promise of a resulting object. This 'work' is never 'realised' in the conventional sense, for the 'object' remains unfinished, in an intermediate stage, while its 'completion', the ending of the process of forming, is marked by the disappearance of the materials out of which it would seem to be comprised. The result of the process is then a series of pictures, a documentation explicitly at one remove from both the materials which were present and the hidden process of forming which led to their removal.

Developed over a period of a year from a 30-minute performance in March 1969 to a full two-hour presentation in March 1970, Rainer's *Continuous Project – Altered Daily* incorporated various kinds of material which by their nature transformed through the process of performance. Constructed of 'interchangeable units'[65] ranging from activities requiring the whole group of six performers to solos, duets and trios, which in their generation had been overseen by Rainer, the piece was an intensely collaborative presentation whose developing shape was determined in each individual performance by the performers themselves. Along with Rainer the group consisted primarily of Becky Arnold, Douglas Dunn, David Gordon, Barbara Lloyd and Steve Paxton, all of whom had been associated with the Judson experiments.

After Morris, Rainer not only relinquished control of her 'materials', the units of performance, but sought to put into question the notion of that which was finished or fully formed. In her detailed programme notes to the final presentation of the *Project* at the Whitney Museum, New York, in April 1970, Rainer set out the contrasting nature of the elements available to the dancers. These are characterised, first, by three 'levels of performance reality':

A. Primary: Performing original material in a personal style.

B. Secondary: Performing someone else's material in a style approximating the original, or working in a known style or 'genre'.

C. Tertiary: Performing someone else's material in a style completely different from, and/or inappropriate to, the original.[66]

In turn, elements available to the piece, and which would be realised in one of these modes, included rehearsal (including discussion and argument), run-through (a polished performance), working out (the creation of new material), surprises (elements introduced without the knowledge of all performers), marking (the performance of material in the absence of conditions necessary to a full presentation), teaching (of one performer by another) and 'behaviour'.

Behaviour could emerge in four specific forms: actual (activities spontaneously occurring in predetermined situations); choreographed (observed and reproduced or stylised behaviour), professional ('the range of gesture and deportment visible in experienced performers'); and amateur ('the range of gesture and deportment visible in inexperienced performers'). For the individual performer, these elements may then again be qualified by their adoption of any of nearly 100 of what Rainer defines as 'roles and metamuscular conditions' which may or may not be visible in 'the execution of physical feats', including:

adolescent
angel
athlete
autistic child
angry child
Annette Michelson
bird
Barbra Streisand
Buster Keaton
brother
Betty Blythe
black militant
confidante
competitor[67]

Rainer's *Project* is evidently analogous to Morris's in important ways. Like Morris, Rainer seeks to withdraw aspects of her own control over the shape or final form of the material with which she works. The material, the elements of Rainer's work, not only finds form through the decisions of the dancers but is subject to shifting and transforming relationships brought about through the process of performing. In this way the act of performance itself provides for the development of 'behaviour' to 'performance', 'surprise' to 'working out', 'rehearsal' to 'run-through' or, potentially, any other development or interpenetration as the act of performance generates behaviours that may be formalised. In fostering such a process of making and transformation, too, the piece looks towards a tension between process and object, as the movement towards an 'object', towards a final form, is staved off and interrupted by the intrusion of new behaviours and incompletions which become subject to transforming levels of performance.

Through these very means, however, Rainer's *Project* also marks itself out as different in character from Morris's. As Morris makes clear, in allowing material to find its own form he looks towards a 'presence' that resists or is beyond a reading of internal relationships between parts. Ironically, though, for Rainer, a retreat as choreographer from the performer's self-determined interactions and development of material is a withdrawal from precisely the kind of controls and disciplines which might stave off a move towards the 'object' in this sense. Free of disciplines or controls, performers tend to interact on levels other than the formal, where a development and interweaving of performance elements, developing tasks, behaviours and references may imply or invite a reading of subject-matters, narratives, even relationships and 'character'. Indeed, Rainer herself clearly provides for this in a vocabulary which offers performers the opportunity to develop interactions through the quotation of style and genre, rehearsal behaviour, including spontaneous and formalised personal interaction, and the possibility of reference to role, character and states of being. Plainly, too, the documentation of the Grand Union's improvisations demonstrates that just such interactions became fundamental to the development of performances, as well as the audience's commitment to them.

In this way Rainer's *Project* looks towards a very different articulation of a tension between process and object than does Morris's work. Rather than resist the reading of internal relationships between figures or parts, Rainer releases the elements of the piece from a rigorous staving off of coherence and developing relationship. In doing so, the piece is allowed to create a space for a reading of continuities and development and yet at the same time acts to disrupt particular readings by the constant shifting and re-formation of that which is being read. Here, the possibility of the 'object', even of an object to be read through developing relationships and events, continually recurs, yet the very freedoms that give rise to the possibility of the object serve also to postpone its actual formation and so its final closure.

Through the *Project* Rainer sets in motion a mechanism for producing change, for promising and pursuing development and variation and at the same time deferring and displacing possible conclusions. Just as the *Project* fosters an active and divergent exchange between its elements, so it looks towards the displacement of one reading by another, a challenging, overlaying and juxtaposition of points of view. In this way, and like that performance which is ostensibly 'minimalist', the *Project* puts into question the possibility of separating the 'work' from its immediate circumstances, and so of identifying those properties which it is in possession of and by which it is defined. The *Project's* very transformation of itself through performance is a reaching toward the contingencies and instabilities of the 'event', an attempt to allow itself to be seen to be penetrated by unstable and unpredictable exchanges and processes. In this way *Continuous Project – Altered Daily* emphasises and makes visible its own contingent nature as *performance*, offering not a 'thing', an 'object', but a series of developing and transforming fragments, displacements and exchanges.

Post-modern dance and the postmodern event

Underlying these various presentations is the notion of a performance which exhibits a dependence upon the occasion of theatre over and above any properties its particular movement-elements, structures or forms might definitively make claim to. In this context, 'dance', like any performance, might be best thought of as a sequence of strategies or bids set in a negotiation over frame, form and content. In these respects, and where it looks towards its own condition, dance comes to an assertion of dependence not independence, of fragmentation and contingency rather than unity and self-sufficiency. Where such work comes to be shadowed and even disrupted by the event of its being read, then it reveals a latent instability, a penetration by its immediate circumstances, and in doing so renders itself uncertain, liable to change. In these instances, post-modern dance can be read as looking toward a postmodern event; an event which shadows and challenges the move toward conclusion, which forces an instability, a vacillation between definition and displacement, and which reveals events, contingencies and negotiations. It is in the context of this notion of a 'postmodern event', too, and of the variety of strategies that may provoke it, that one might most usefully return to that work which can be set directly against a 'postmodern style'.

Chapter 6

Telling Stories: Narrative Against Itself

> The response we make when we 'believe' a work of the imagination is that of saying: 'This is the way things are. I have always known it without being fully aware that I knew it. Now in the presence of this play or novel or poem (or picture or piece of music) I know that I know it.'[1]

In its presentation at the Performing Garage in New York, the Wooster Group's *Route 1 & 9 (The Last Act)* begins with 'THE LESSON (Upstairs): In Which a Man Delivers a Lecture on the Structure and Meaning of *Our Town*', the screening of a reconstruction of an *Encyclopaedia Britannica* 'teaching film' in which Clifton Fadiman introduces Thornton Wilder's play *Our Town* (1938). After Fadiman, Ron Vawter of the Wooster Group sets out 'Mr Wilder's art', demonstrating what he sees as the experience *Our Town* instils in its audience. Through an explication of Wilder's 'use of music, theme and variation, and of the condensed line or word',[2] Vawter traces the play's gentle reminder, through its portrait of the community of Grover's Corner, of the deeper 'truths' that underlie everyday experience.

In the Wooster Group's reconstruction, however, and while Vawter faithfully re-presents Fadiman's demonstration of the means by which Wilder's play 'helps us to understand and accept our existence upon the earth',[3] the language and construction of the 'teaching film' have been displaced. As the critic attempts to draw the viewer toward his own self-assured point of view, the tape sets out a subtle exaggeration of the means by which he gathers authority to himself and is framed by the film. The camera, David Savran notes, 'holds long static shots of the lecturer and pans portentously as he moves back and forth'.[4] As the lecture continues it 'zooms in for important "truths" and underscores them by spelling out catch phrases across the bottom of the television screen'.[5]

Here, and despite the fact that Vawter carefully gives voice to Fadiman's argument, the meaning and efficacy of the teaching film are put into question, as the Wooster Group shadow Fadiman's explication of *Our Town* with their own explication of his lecture. The result is doubly ironic. In analysing and revealing the purposes and effects of Fadiman's film, the Wooster Group show it to be a project with its own character and purpose, so setting it at a distance from its object. Paradoxically, though, in doing this they implicitly put the veracity of their own reproduction of Fadiman's film into question. Like Fadiman's lecture, the Wooster Group's tape speaks for its object by reconstructing it. In pointing toward Fadiman's displacement of that which he would speak for, then, his presentation of a 'simulation' which reveals what *Our Town* 'really means', so the Wooster Group draw attention to their own displacement of Fadiman's argument, their own participation in precisely such a project. In such a way, the Wooster Group's exercise not only mounts a critique of Fadiman's film but implicitly turns back against itself.

Through such means, the Wooster Group move in the opposite direction from the consensus the lecturer would seek to engender. Far from simply contradicting or opposing Fadiman's argument, which would only look towards another form of consensus, their re-presentation exposes and disrupts the means by which such agreements would be fostered, either by Fadiman or themselves. The result is a strategy that looks towards the uncertainties and instabilities suppressed by the lecturer's attempt to draw the audience towards that which 'we all know'. It is a strategy that fosters contention, that places itself into question just as it questions its object, that gives rise to conflicts and contradictions it does not offer to resolve.

Ambivalence and transgression: the Wooster Group and Karen Finley

In the controversy over *Route 1 & 9*, one of the things that was said was, 'There's no distance on it.' In other words, it was racist, because there wasn't a character or voice of authority saying, 'Look, this is a horrible thing. This is racist.' I suspect that if Spalding had been off to the side saying, in one way or another, 'I deplore this,' it would have been alright. Everyone would have said, 'Oh, this guy is dealing with his racism on the stage,' instead of the audience really having to deal with the racism unmediated.[6]

The Wooster Group's treatment of Fadiman's film exemplifies the equivocal attitude inscribed within their treatment of the various elements their work brings into collision. In *Route 1 & 9* these elements included the 'teaching film', extracts from *Our Town*, blackface routines once performed by the black comedian Pigmeat Markham, comedy-horror sequences as well as a pornographic tape. According to LeCompte, her interest in the Encyclopedia Britannica film, as with *Our Town* itself, was rooted in the ambivalent nature of her response to it. In conversation with David Savran, she recalled that:

I liked the Clifton Fadiman film, but was bothered about liking it. It touched nostalgic chords of comfort for me that made me angry. It pressed two buttons simultaneously. And I found myself unable to accept either in comfort. I couldn't destroy it and I couldn't go with it and be satisfied. I wanted to dig more deeply into it.[7]

Ostensibly concerned with the community of Grover's Corner, a small town in turn-of-the-century New Hampshire, *Our Town* focuses upon two families, the Webbs and the Gibbs, whose children, Emily and George, promise themselves to each other in childhood, marry, and are parted by Emily's death in childbirth. Act one, 'Daily Life', contemplates the character of Grover's Corner and its community. Act two, 'Love and Marriage', brings the community together for the day of Emily and George's wedding. Act three, set on the day of Emily's funeral, places Emily amongst the dead, allowing her to reflect upon her life as she waits 'for the eternal part ... to come out clear'.[8]

Mediating between these fragments, and between the audience and the play, a Stage-Manager acts as narrator, manipulating the few items of scenery the play demands while setting its events in a broadening context. Speaking in past, present and future tenses concurrently, he traces events, experiences and desires which seem to find themselves repeated through and despite change; experiences which, by dint of their very ordinariness and familiarity, might transcend history and culture. Finally, in act three, the Stage-Manager draws the audience toward the realisation that:

we all know that *something* is eternal. And it ain't houses and it ain't names, and it ain't earth, and it ain't even the stars ... everybody knows in their bones that something is eternal, and that something has to do with human beings ... there's something way down deep that's eternal about every human being.[9]

Emphasising, after Gertrude Stein, the 'perpetual present' of action in the theatre, Wilder sought a 'new drama' that would escape from what he saw as naturalism's 'devitalizing' emphasis upon 'place', upon 'specification and localization'.[10] Yet in breaching fourth-wall illusionism, Wilder pursued not the overtly fragmented vision of much modern art and literature but a form of work that could give direct voice to a deeper unity underlying all experience. To this end, Wilder sought to liberate theatre from what he saw as a concern for simple happenstance in order that it might realise its capacity to carry 'the art of narration to a higher power than the novel or epic poem'.[11] *Our Town* exemplifies the combination of these elements, its strength lying, in Wilder's terms, not in the veracity of particular incidents but 'in the succession of events ... in the unfolding of an idea'.[12] Indeed, the importance of the particular incidents within *Our Town* lies not so much in their individual weight as in the fact that they are commonplace, a fact which, seen through the metaphysical framework the Stage-Manager weaves, ties them to underlying and universal patterns and experiences.

In act three, then, it is through Emily's reflection upon what has passed that the value of even the most ordinary moments of life is most clearly articulated. For Emily, death does not mean the simple fulfilment of that which underlay and was promised by life but, as her passions drain from her, an understanding of the blindness of the living to the value and vibrancy of every moment of life. Revisiting the living, this realisation only brings her pain and she is forced to retreat from the ignorance of those she has left behind. Returning to the grave, Emily laments, 'Oh earth, you're too wonderful for anyone to realize you', asking, finally, 'Do any human beings ever realize life while they live it? – every, every minute?'[13]

With the end of 'THE LESSON (Upstairs)', the audience moves below into the performance space itself. Here, the first live sequence begins, and Part One of *Route 1 and 9* continues with 'THE LESSON (Downstairs): In Which the Stage Hands Arrange the Stage for the Last Act of *Our Town*'. Now, two white performers present the first of a number of blackface sequences. In heavy makeup and blinded by their overtly blacked-out sunglasses they take on the mantle of Wilder's

Stage-Manager, attempting to construct a forced-perspective, skeletal house which will act as the set for the last act of *Our Town* and which forms part three of *Route 1 & 9*. Moving clumsily around the space and near the audience they develop a slapstick double-act, while instructions for building the house and a routine between two (apparently black-faced) actors plays over loudspeakers.

With the construction of the house underway a few feet before the audience, a brief blackout signals the beginning of Part Two, 'THE PARTY: In Which the Stage Hands Call it a Day and a Telegram is Sent'. While the four televisions suspended above the performance area offer a panoramic view of the Manhattan skyline, the men continue to build. Two white women in blackface enter and, as 'Annie' and 'Willie', make a series of live telephone calls to order food for Annie's birthday party. Following a final call to 'Kenny' and 'Pigmeat', the two male performers transform into guests at the party and the performance itself shifts gear:

> Now transformed, the men pick up the liquor and join the women for the birthday party. 'ALL RIGHT LET'S GO,' Willie yells as the song *Hole in the Wall* explodes over the speakers. There follows the re-enactment of the Pigmeat Markham routine ... a wildly theatrical revel, a vaudeville of comedy and dance.[14]

As the party continues two more performers enter and, as Kenny and Pigmeat, perform a reconstruction of a Markham comedy routine from the 1960s. Armed with outsized bottles of rye and (mistakenly) castor oil, they joke, shout and pour drink on the floor, toasting each other over the music and dancing. As the music continues, Savran recounts, the performers stop one by one, 'because each has to go "send a telegram" ', the meaning of which becomes clear 'when Pig defecates in his pants', providing the sequence with its punchline:

> PIG: Oh, me.
> WILLIE: Pigmeat.
> PIG: Oh, ho, ho, oh ho.
> . . . .
> WILLIE: Whatsa matter Pigmeat?
> PIG: Whadya mean?
> WILLIE: Don't tell me you gotta send a telegram too?
> PIG: No, no, I done sent mine.[15]

As this sequence ends the performers quieten and the focus of the piece shifts to the four video monitors raised 14 feet above the stage-floor. Once lowered to their foreground position, seven feet above the ground, extracts from the last act of *Our Town* begin to play simultaneously across all four monitors. With this, Part Three, 'THE LAST ACT (The Cemetery Scene): In Which Four Chairs are Placed on the Stage Facing the Audience to Represent Graves', begins. As fragments from *Our Town* draw the audience's attention, the blackface performers move quietly around the darkened stage engaging in a variety of tasks and interactions while trying not to distract the audience. As the action develops the blackface performers come to mimic not simply the calming tones of *Our Town* but Emily's reliving of her twelfth birthday. While Emily recounts the details of her party, the performers quietly play through Annie's birthday in the skeletal house. When Emily receives her birthday gift, Annie 'shows up wearing an extravagant blue-silk creation'.[16] At some point the men cross-dress, pulling dresses over their suits. As the fragments of *Our Town* come to an end, the party asserts itself once again. With Emily's closing lines another blackface routine forcefully disrupts the calm with a 'Ghoul Dance', a grotesque parody of Wilder's vision of the after-life:

> Suddenly 'Jump the Line' sounds and the four, in what remains of their blackface, begin to dance furiously, shaking their skirts wildly, a horrible grimace on their faces. They approach the audience, blood streaming down their faces, their mouths gaping open to reveal vampire fangs.[17]

Finally, with the abrupt end of the routine, the performers sit passively, avoiding eye contact with the audience, and the beginning of Part Four, 'ROUTE 1 & 9', is signalled as three video tapes are shown simultaneously. On the upper monitors, now raised again high above the floor, are two tapes of the same sequence, 'In Which a Van Picks Up Two Hitchhikers and Heads South'. Here LeCompte drives a van out of the city, her male passenger smoking and drinking coffee. At some point in the journey the van stops and picks up a hitchhiking couple. Meanwhile at stage level, in the skeletal house, an old black-and-white television shows a third tape in which

> the performers who played the hitchhikers are going through a series of sexual turns ... The sex sequences are graphic, the couple trying

various positions. They are less concerned with performing for the camera than with allowing it to oversee them, much like a voyeur.[18]

As the videos end so *Route 1 & 9* comes to a close.

Self-evidently, read against *Our Town*, the collisions of texts and images which make up *Route 1 & 9* serve to violate the parameters and qualities of Wilder's vision. By taking Wilder's maxim to realise the value of each present moment literally and uncritically, *Route 1 and 9* would seem to reveal and parody the narrow parameters of *Our Town*'s image of the 'universal'. Through the blackface the Wooster Group present much of what the inhabitants of Grover's Corner define themselves against, and which is represented in this denigrating image of the 'other'; a violent expression of physical vitality and energy, a celebration of sexuality and danger, a revelling in the body rather than the spirit. The pornographic tape similarly and graphically points toward the repressions upon which the 'innocence' of the community may rest, and which is given voice momentarily in Emily's apprehension at her marriage. Formally, too, *Route 1 & 9* explodes the hierarchies upon which Wilder's vision depends. In the Group's work, LeCompte suggests, 'the core is always dispersed',[19] while a combination and juxtaposition of radically different elements serves to undermine any single reading that might be made of the piece. It might follow that in opposition to *Our Town*, and rather than assert the 'right' perspective, *Route 1 & 9* emphasises conflict and difference, creating contentious and ambiguous relationships between values and perspectives that are resistant to any easy reading and resolution. By implication, the single most unequivocal critique of *Our Town*, as with Fadiman's lecture, then, may be its assumption of the right to such a 'totalising' view within which everything must find its place or be excluded.

Clearly, though, this conflict between perspectives and texts resists not only the assumptions inscribed within *Our Town* but also a reading based on such a simple opposition. Vawter's lecture, for example, not only questions the ground of Fadiman's authority but its own, while Fadiman's argument is rehearsed and offered all the same. Similarly, while the blackface may be read as an attack on the narrow confines of Wilder's vision of a small-town, white America, it does so while being held within denigrating representations of black people. At once, then, the blackface challenges *Our Town*'s hegemony while condemning the white performers to re-enact its exclusivity before the Group's predominantly white, middle-class audience. Touching on the ironies of this position, LeCompte has acknowledged the double-edged nature of the image, arguing that for a white audience it 'is both ... a painful representation of blacks and also wild, joyous, and nihilistic and, therefore, freeing'.[20] Similarly, the pornographic tape hardly offers itself as an unequivocal release from the repressions it points toward. While, as Ron Vawter suggests, the presence of the tape may serve to set 'a little pro-creative act'[21] against Wilder's graveyard, it also remains an overtly and deliberately pornographic presentation[22] open to charges of abuse and obscenity.

Such ironies intrude upon each of the elements out of which *Route 1 & 9* is made up, as found material is wrong-footed or undercut through its reproduction. According to LeCompte, one key to the process by which the performance is compiled is a self-conscious reframing of found elements. She notes:

> When they act I use acting. When they perform, I use that. I frame other people's style in my frame so that it says something I want it to. I use their work in terms of the frame/context of the piece, which I set.[23]

In this way not only is a vocabulary of sharply contrasting styles and modes of work fostered within a single performance, but individual elements are placed on an ambivalent footing. In so far as a 'found' element or sequence is reproduced, the performance remains complicit with that which it reproduces. Yet the very fact of the material's reproduction puts it into question, as does its simultaneous and concurrent juxtaposition with like and unlike elements.

Specific strategies which LeCompte and the performers variously adopt extend this process, evidencing the displacement of material from the ground on which some aspect of its transparency, authority and so meaning depended. The first blackface routines, the comic building sequences, are placed on uncertain ground by the very fact of the performers' blindness. While clearly a source of much of the comedy, their handicap also slows the performance down, creating a tension between the routine and its painful pace and repetition, forcing a shifting and difficult relationship between the audience and the comedy. Similar tensions are also present in the readings of *Our Town*. LeCompte notes that as the group began to work with Wilder's text:

> I realised that when you took the Stage-Manager out of *Our Town*, it became a soap opera. So I took the last act and worked with Willem on separating it into scenes, close-up scenes with a soap opera feel.

We did improvs around a soap opera style, using TVs ... And from that we got a kind of rhythm. The actor's pacing is soap opera but the visual image is more 'portraiture', the actors speaking directly to the camera which serves as point of view.[24]

In this version of the cemetery scene, Wilder's representations are broken free of the Stage-Manager's narrative, while the actors' style of performance and the 'scenes' chosen offer a deliberately reductive view of the play. The visual image of 'portraiture' clarifies the tensions this treatment gives rise to. These close-ups seem to go too far, forcing the actor into an introverted, conversational mode, while creating a sense of entrapment or intrusion into the personal, the private. Reframed in this way, Wilder's representations of everyday life take on soap opera's overbearing concern for the ordinary and the trivial, seeming to give everyday events an attention and so significance they cannot bear. Ironically, in the absence of the Stage-Manager's explanations, Emily's reflections on her life seem confined to an intense and single-minded concern with precisely the idiosyncratic events Wilder set out to see beyond.

Such ironies are exacerbated by the juxtaposition of elements treated in this way. Constructed largely through a collage of found texts, actions and images, the Wooster Group would seem to put the formal and thematic boundaries of their performances into question. In a collage where 'Everything is equally weighted',[25] the resolution of a conflict between quotations, re-presentations and adaptations is staved off by their resistance to being read through each other. The very fact that such material is recognisably 'found' material, that it makes reference to 'other' histories and identities, aspects that the performance has not or cannot fully assimilate, leaves it in a sense unsorted, open to question in its relevance and consequence. The result is an open intertextuality, where the internal, self-supporting integrity of the 'work' is given over to a presentation which repeatedly sites itself in relation to pre-existing texts from whose vantage points elements of the collage may be variously read.

The significance of this becomes clearer in the effect of the blackface. In the context of *Route 1 & 9* this equivocal figure, which, historically, has been employed both to reinforce and subvert racial stereotype,[26] becomes subject to competing points of view. The reversals brought about through the blackface house-building, party and ghoul dance may be read as representing the blackface as that which *Our Town* excludes. In their re-enactment by white performers, however, the blackface routines might be taken as an *act* of exclusion, the presentation of images not sufficiently distanced from the denigration they recall and continue to rehearse. After the New York State Council on the Arts (NYSCA) and other critics of the piece, one might cite the live telephone calls as a wilful confusion of crude caricature and the quotation and contextualisation of a theatrical image. Indeed, this very reading of the piece reputedly cost the Wooster Group some 40 per cent of their grant funding from the NYSCA.[27]

While the stubborn independence of the individual elements and texts foster such conflicting readings, the Wooster Group themselves frame their performances in such a way as to call into question their independence from one another. *Route 1 & 9*, the Group make clear, is Part One of a trilogy, *The Road to Immortality*, of which *L.S.D. (... Just the High Points ...)* (1984) forms Part Two, while *Frank Dell's The Temptation of Saint Anthony* (1987) comprises Part Three. This trilogy follows the pattern established by their first sequence of pieces, *Three Places in Rhode Island*, which consisted of *Sakonnet Point* (1975), *Rumstick Road* (1977), *Nyatt School* (1978) and *Point Judith (An Epilogue)* (1979). Only the short dance pieces *Hula* (1981) and *For the Good Times* (1983) along with the play *North Atlantic* (1984) have fallen outside this pattern. For LeCompte, it seems, such sequences reflect and grow out of the fact that the perspective from which choices are made shifts and may be turned back on itself. In self-consciously seeking to create a body of work, LeCompte would appear not to elaborate a particular position or developing argument so much as deliberately attack or remake her own vocabulary. She notes that 'I'm always remaking the vocabulary, constantly rewriting it. Things are reversed and totally destroyed, and we go back on what we did in previous pieces.'[28]

Consistently with this the blackface recurs in Part Two of *L.S.D.* in which, initially, the Group performed an hysterical 30-minute rendering of *The Crucible*, later replaced by Michael Kirby's play *The Hearing* following the intervention of Arthur Miller.[29] Here, the Group implicitly set their own 'transgression' in *Route 1 & 9* against Miller's treatment of Tituba, the black servant. Through their presentation of a black role conventionally played by a black actress by a white performer in blackface, the Wooster Group mount a critique of both Miller's unselfconscious reference to stereotype and an unthinking acceptance of this treatment and its implications. In turn, as the white performer goes on to play 'white' roles while still wearing the remnants of her blackface makeup, the conventional meanings and references of the blackface are challenged through an overt disjunction between its history and the roles the blackfaced performer takes up.

Here, then, the reworking of material serves to heighten the uncertainties the process of reframing and the conflict between texts fosters. As readings multiply and turn back on each other, this 'body of work' enters into conflict with itself. According to Ron Vawter, one key to the performances lies in precisely the way in which elements are combined to create a space open to meanings of various kinds:

> An event which can be interpreted only one way inhibits and limits the possibility. It's not that we're deliberately trying to make pieces which are mute. Just the opposite. I often see a piece as an opportunity for meaning, rather than an expression of a single meaning.[30]

Such strategies not only put into question that material which is incorporated or reproduced but, through the construction and displacement of perspectives, provoke conflicts and contradictions which unsettle or interrupt moves toward a single reading or point of view. At the same time, though, and despite the overtly social and political reference much of this material makes, this resistance to unity and synthesis also effects a resistance to the giving of social and political *meaning*. In this respect, *Route 1 & 9* may be identified with formal strategies through which the process of negotiation, the move towards meaning, is exposed, and where the meaning of particular images is disrupted, postponed, staved off. In doing so, however, it seems that *Route 1 & 9* risks pursuing a confusion of the politically radical and the reactionary or, at least, a deliberate provocation of a conflict between these two possibilities. Such a presentation inevitably becomes uncomfortable, by its nature open to charges of an unthinking complicity with the material it incorporates.

Perhaps even more so than the Wooster Group, Karen Finley's appropriations of languages of abuse, denigration and pornography have provoked a sharply divided critical and popular response. Since *The Constant State of Desire* (1986), in particular, Finley's work has been read both as a capitulation to male violence and objectification, and a powerful transgression and challenge to the construction of sexual difference.[31] More controversially, the piece has been condemned, despite acknowledgements of Finley's 'feminist intentions', first as an exploitation of the popular taste for obscenity and secondly for relying on arcane references to feminist theory incapable of 'full comprehension' by the 'average' spectator.[32]

The Constant State of Desire is typical of the fractured nature of Finley's performances, consisting of a series of monologues punctuated

by improvised exchanges with the audience. Her published text[33] breaks
the piece down into five sections: *Strangling Baby Birds*, *Enter Entrepreneur*, *Two Stories*, *Common Sense* and *The Father in All of Us*. As in
much of Finley's other work, these stories intertwine painful descriptions of sexual abuse with, by turns, an angry and despairing mourning
for the dying implicitly bound up with the consequences of AIDS. In the
course of this, Finley's concerns spill over towards racism and the abuse
of minorities, to the abandonment of the homeless, of addicts, and to the
marginalised. In her later monologue, *We Keep Our Victims Ready*
(1990), these broader political concerns become explicit as accounts of
sexual abuse, the persecution of AIDS victims and of artists themselves
are set against images of the Nazi death camps.

Rather than offer a coherent critique of a process of marginalisation,
or of sexual objectification, subordination and abuse, however, Finley's
performances operate first and foremost on a direct and powerful emotional level, though by no means one which is straightforwardly cath-
artic. In particular, Finley's appropriations of pornographic imagery and
language serve to call into question not only the distance and perspective an audience might wish to establish in an address to such material,
but her own implication in the processes of objectification and abuse she
ostensibly attacks.

The Constant State of Desire begins with the recollection of a woman's dreams; she imagines killing baby birds, an image which slips
quickly into that of the woman herself caged and watched over by her
family. The dream is then a dream of falling and of crying without being
able to give voice, and one, like others of being beaten and tortured, that
is given importance and picked over by doctors: 'the same doctors who
anaesthetized her during the birth of her children .... who called her an
animal as she nursed ... who gave her episiotomies. No more sexual
feelings for her during and after childbirth.'[34]

The monologue rapidly turns toward self-blame, however, and, now
in the first person, present tense, to a mourning of the death of television
stars, the suicide of her father, the report of an abortion and an incestu-
ous rape. The father committed suicide, Finley reports, 'because he no
longer found me attractive'. She concludes, 'you can tell that I prefer
talking about the fear of living, as opposed to the fear of dying'.[35]

With this the tack of Finley's text shifts again. In performance, Finley
takes off her clothes, smashes eggs in a clear plastic bag and then uses a
child's soft toy as an applicator to smear the yellow liquid over herself.
Finally she sprinkles glitter and confetti over her body and wraps
herself in paper boas.[36] This completed, the second monologue, *Enter*

Entrepreneur, signals a vitriolic attack on the art-consuming yuppie, mapping out his consumption of abuse as art and culminating in a vivid description of the castration of Wall Street traders who 'don't miss their balls 'cause they're too busy fucking me with everything else they got'.[37] Finley completes her 'sweet revenge' by boiling their testicles, rolling them in dung and selling them as 'Easter eggs to gourmet chocolate shops'.[38]

Two Stories shifts the ground again, recounting the abuse of a woman by her husband and setting this against a sexual assault by burglars 'at gunpoint in front of her own children and pets'.[39] This in turn slips into an account, in the first person, present tense, of a son's resentment of his father's rejection of him as he leaves for Vietnam. *Common Sense* then initiates an attack on Freud, which moves toward a more overtly political account of women's exclusion, marginalisation and a self-destructive internalisation of these processes. Finally, Freud is inverted as Finley traces the archetypal father's jealousy 'when he discovered woman's ability to have multiple orgasms'.[40] Finley teases the men in her audience: 'Okay, I know that some of you guys like to let us know that you can fuck more than once. But I need no time to refuel. *So maybe it's womb envy instead of penis envy.*'[41]

In her final monologue, *The Father in All of Us*, which is divided into several parts, Finley readdresses the concerns running through the piece but in a more graphic and difficult way. 'My First Sexual Experience' sets out a violent parody of the privileging of Oedipal drives and desires and the definition of woman in terms of lack. The piece begins with Finley's description of birth itself as a sexual experience, after which she takes on the mantle of a male 'motherfucker' who uses a baby as a substitute penis to abuse his indifferent mother. This is followed by 'Refrigerator', which returns to a description of sexual abuse, setting out a distressing account of a father's assault on his daughter. Sitting her in the refrigerator:

> he leans down to the vegetable bin, opens it and takes out the carrots, the celery, the zucchini, the cucumbers. Then he starts working on my little hole, my little, little, hole. My little girl hole. Showing me 'what it's like to be mamma' ... Next thing I know I'm in bed crying, bleeding. I got all my dollies and animals around me. I've got Band-Aids between their legs. If they can't protect me, I'll protect them.[42]

'The Father in All of Us' then turns explicitly to AIDS as Finley again gives voice to the son whose sexuality and death is rejected by his father. Images of violent sexual abuse are then set against accounts of addicts and the homeless abandoned on the street. Finally, in a gentler tone but no less bitter a parody, Finley speaks as a yuppy in search of a 'religious experience', but who finds only dying friends and a 'White Man's Guilt', a self-indulgent discomfort borne of exploitation and privilege.

Like *Route 1 & 9, The Constant State of Desire* is constructed through shifting perspectives, while Finley's relationship to the material she engages with remains an ambivalent one. Through her rehearsal of violent and even pornographic imagery and language, Finley couches her performance and her presentation of herself in the terms of a violent sexual objectification and abuse. Paradoxically, and despite her verbal assaults on the abusers, Finley's performances have been read as capitulating through the very terms by which she tells her stories with that which she bitterly attacks. Indeed, one may even argue that any such engagement can only be politically self-destructive as, by its nature, an appropriation of male languages of objectification and abuse speaks to a male audience first and is bound in its reception by the assumptions that generate and sustain its terms. For a critic such as Jill Dolan, powerful as Finley's performance evidently are, they remain limited, even self-defeating:

> There is not much potential for radical change in Finley's work because ... she is still caught within the representational system to which she refers. Although male spectators are challenged and confronted in Finley's work, her aims are achieved by abusing herself under representational terms that remain operative from the male point of view. Finley perverts the strippers position, but remains defined by its traditional history.[43]

Yet the very extreme and surprising nature of Finley's appropriations, as well as the shifting and fragmented nature of her monologues, can be read as resisting such an accommodation. Far from offering herself as a passive object, Finley takes on and incorporates these languages into her performance in such a way that she becomes active through them. Here, one can argue, by re-enacting the violence of the male subject she subverts the terms of his objectification, appropriating the language that would define her as a passive victim and throwing it back at her audience. Importantly, too, as she engages in this process Finley effects a continual change of ground and identity, taking on and disposing, variously and unpredictably, of male and female voices, and the personas of

abused, abuser, victim and protagonist. In doing so, she overtly resists
the spectator's reading of 'character' as a unifying force, and particularly a reading of herself as an empathetic figure or victim in relation to
which the various experiences she recounts might be placed.

In performance, the tensions between these poles become even more
apparent, as Finley's shifts of narrative voice and the clash between
texts are themselves framed within improvised and revealing exchanges
with the audience.[44] This rapport looks toward a dual effect, at once
standing in tension with the aggressive and sometimes abusive nature
of her monologues while evidencing the process of her performance,
the construction of the 'act' itself. At the time of her performance of
The Constant State of Desire Finley articulated this tension, making a
distinction in her work between 'experimental theatre', material which
had become fixed and was repeatable, and a 'performance procedure'
which can be prepared for but is not rehearsed.[45]

Caught between these two poles, Finley's performances of her monologues set themselves against conventional theatrical and dramatic criteria. Indeed, in important respects it is more appropriate to read
Finley's performance against Body Art's exposure of the physical and
psychological vulnerability of the artist or a concern with a process of
making than the actor's realisation of a text. Charged with presenting a
'bad' performance, Finley has responded by arguing that in such circumstances the exposure of her own struggle to perform becomes part
of her subject-matter:

> for that reason I thought it was the best night: people could see me as
> I am. I showed that a performance is really hard to do. I think it's my
> duty as a performer to be completely honest, to show them what I'm
> going through.[46]

Such a reading of Finley's performance begins to turn away from an
attention simply to the material she appropriates and towards a framing
and treatment of this material through formal strategies. From this point
of view, and while the influences acting on the Wooster Group and
Karen Finley are diverse, their work can be usefully set against treatments of narrative defined through self-conscious appropriations of conventional theatre forms and figures. Here, narrative is treated as a figure
with certain formal consequences, and one whose effect is to be questioned through its displacement in an address to its place and effect in an
active negotiation over identity and meaning.

Resisting narrative

Yvonne Rainer's final theatre-piece was a two-hour multi-media performance, *This is the story of a woman who...*, first presented in March 1973.
Like *Grand Union Dreams* and her film *Lives of Performers* of 1972,
which marked the culmination of her work with the Grand Union, this
presentation pursued the increasingly open address to dramatic convention that characterised the development of her work through performance and toward an exclusive concern with film. Yet despite open
references to narrative, 'persona', and an interaction between 'characters',
in this work Rainer's use of conventional form and figure is always
qualified by a displacement or subversion of the continuities such elements would seem to look towards.

Set in a simply defined rectangular space, *This is the story of a
woman who ...* incorporates film and slide projections, before which the
three performers, originally Rainer herself, Shirley Soffer and John
Erdman, variously interact with each other and tell their stories to the
audience. While Rainer and Erdman alternate between sitting on a pair
of chairs at the rear, interacting with each other around the space and
on a mattress placed downstage right, Soffer sits before a microphone
near the audience, ostensibly taking on the role of narrator.

Soffer's entry signals the beginning of the piece. As she takes her seat
behind the microphone thunder is heard, then the sound of rain. As the
rain sounds, one of three projections that may be made in sequence or
simultaneously across the back wall shows Soffer in what seems to be
various family photographs. The photographs are replaced by a title,
'Inner Appearances', which cues Erdman's entry. At first singing to himself, Erdman vacuums the space and a sequence of 15 texts are projected
in a broken rhythm. Sporadically, Erdman interrupts his task to stand
still or sit on a chair or the mattress. The sense of time, Rainer suggests,
'is protracted and melancholy'.[47] The texts offer what seem to be self-
conscious and discontinuous accounts of Erdman's thoughts, but ones
that are in the third person and that weave in and out of an implied fictional context. They reflect on 'the character's mask', his 'growing irri-
tation', the fact that 'before the performance he ran into someone he
hadn't seen for a year'.[48] In turn, this meeting is absorbed into a narrative in which Erdman has been left by his wife or lover. The text recounts
an incident in which 'the character' hides in a doorway to avoid the new
couple. Finally, Erdman sits on a chair at the rear and the text concludes
by putting itself into question: 'Cliché is, in a sense, the purest art of
intelligibility; it tempts us with the possibility of enclosing life within

beautifully unalterable formulas, of obscuring the arbitrary nature of imagination with an appearance of necessity.'[49]

As the piece continues to unfold, various narrative voices intrude unpredictably upon one another. While Soffer, sitting before the microphone, remains silent, a tape of Erdman's voice plays, offering an account of a woman's loss, possibly her feelings at being left by her partner. Soffer takes over the narrative, describing a scene from a relationship, an exchange rooted in suspicion. Meanwhile, Rainer and Erdman develop a sequence of 'stop-motion poses in relation to each other and the objects'.[50] The lights fade and the text returns, describing both a breaking up and a reconciliation. Soffer reads the first four of nine 'paragraphs' which she announces as such and numbers them. She recounts a woman's visit to the Pantheon, a cathedral, against projected illustrations of cities, gardens and anonymous places. Fragments of incidents or experiences unfold variously. The slide projections offer dialogue as a film of an ocean and beach is superimposed over the left-hand slide image; Soffer delivers a monologue in the first person, present tense of being lost in a city, the victim of unwanted attentions. As Rainer and Erdman enact a slow-motion fight scene, the distinctions between narrative lines and identities threaten to be further confused as Soffer steps into the performance space proper:

> Shirley stands downstage centre with microphone and says 'That's her fantasy. If it were mine I'd do it differently.' She has a screaming fit, then says, 'I just can't do it tonight.' John starts to rearrange the chairs. Shirley goes to him and says 'Her unrelenting inten ...' Yvonne looks up from where she has been shuffling papers, stands up, coughs, watches Shirley lie down on the mattress.[51]

In this way, the elements constituting the performance continually invite a reading of narrative continuity and yet resist the actual construction of a single or even predominant narrative. Ironically, this disruption of the reading of narrative is achieved first of all through the clear and specific claim of each narrative voice. In this piece, individual voices and texts re-narrativise each other, either directly or through the redrawing of analogous events, experiences and themes. As if to compound this, the particular identity of these voices proves to be elusive. Repeatedly, what is narrated are the experiences, feelings and points of view of the 'other', which may or may not be Rainer, Erdman or Soffer's 'characters'. Thematically, this may be read as an evasion of responsibility, a measuring of one's own actions in terms of another's. Formally, however, it means that the narrative voice fails to identify its own position, but concerns itself with redrawing the position of others. Paradoxically, only Soffer, as the external voice of the 'narrator', speaks of herself directly, intruding, at this point, into that which she would ostensibly draw a frame around and lead the audience through.

The equivocal nature of this invitation to read the 'story' of a woman or her experiences is echoed, too, in the relationship between narrative and the performers' actions and interactions. In the first scene, incorporating Erdman's 'dance' *Inner Appearances*, Rainer suggests, 'The dance consisted of cleaning, vacuuming the performance space. Drama and psychological meaning were conveyed by slides of typescript dealing with the state of mind of a character ... The dancer becomes a persona related by spatial proximity to the projected texts.'[52]

Erdman presents his dance while his proximity to the projected texts invites a reading of the dancer as 'persona'. The nature of the text, which announces its own construction of a fiction and use of cliché, at once extends an invitation to read his presence through its terms and yet maintains a self-conscious distance from Erdman's activities. Typically, this scene does not offer unequivocal representations of character or dramatic incident but actions, texts, images and commentaries which stand in self-conscious, uncertain and shifting relationships to one another.

As the piece continues, and once Soffer has joined Rainer and Erdman, the conflict between the status and nature of the narrative voices intensifies. As Soffer engages directly with the two 'characters', a tape of Rainer's voice seems to take on what was Soffer's role. In turn, a film of Soffer in bed further draws her into the relationship that seemed to be Rainer and Erdman's. Finally, the text 'She showed him her dance', signals the incorporation of a series of overt quotations into the piece. Rainer performs an earlier dance-piece, *Three Satie Spoons*; 40 stills of the shower scene from Hitchcock's *Psycho* are set against 'paragraph seven', in which Soffer tells the story of a woman leaving, nauseated, from a film-theatre. Rainer and Erdman make a series of approaches to each other against a text which concludes by falling overtly into cliché: 'His performance was magnificent. Afterwards she wept. Then she slept. As a pool of warm water spreading in the sunlight.'[53]

The intrusion of such quotations and references extend and intensify the series of displacements the narrative voices effect. The 'cliché' Rainer's texts incorporate may advance the 'story' and its meanings, yet, as they do so, they declare themselves to be second hand, formulaic. Rainer's overt appropriations offer similar positions from which readings may be at once made and questioned. The sequence from *Psycho* may parallel or parody the 'woman's' experiences, inviting a re-reading of a relationship or her partner's actions, or even be taken as a fantasy or dream. Prefaced and shadowed by the text, 'She shows him her dance', Rainer's performance of *Three Satie Spoons* gains a new ambiguity, perhaps offering itself as a metaphor for some kind of exchange between them. Whatever readings these elements invite or accommodate, however, they pointedly resist incorporation into a formal or thematic whole both by their obvious *difference*, their formal and stylistic independence from the elements in relation to which they are placed, and by the histories and references they bring with them.

In this piece, then, Rainer's elements repeatedly invite the reading of a narrative. At the same time, though, the sequence of claim and counter-claim, of parallel and reversal, within which these narrative appropriations and conventions are bound, continually undercut and dis-place the ground on which such a narrative might be followed through. Here, ironically, it is the very narrative voices that invite a reading of the piece in terms of an unfolding whole that resist integration into such a whole, that speak for others and will not be spoken for.

In fact, for Rainer, it seems that the more such figures come into play, the more sharply their unifying effect should be resisted. Rainer has argued that 'the more meanings get spelled out for an audience in terms of specific narrative information, the stronger the need for 'opening up' things at another level with ambiguous or even ambivalent clues and signs'.[54] As narrative strategies emerge and develop in Rainer's work, so the particular narrative comes to be shadowed by that which it cannot encompass. Competing narrative voices displace one another, to be exposed as figures which would establish a continuity through which the 'other' would be silenced or spoken for. Narrative patterns are revealed by events which escape their logic, undermining the transparency of cause-and-effect. Overt quotations intrude formally and thematically, setting the narratives against which they are placed in relation to others beyond the piece itself.

Rainer's late performances offer examples of a range of work that in incorporating narrative comes to interrogate the nature and consequence of the act of narration. Here, the reading of representation and continuity is at once invited and disrupted, as the act of narration is revealed to be the act of reading one element through another, of having one voice speak for another.

For Joan Jonas, whose early performances had been linked to the aftermath of the Judson experiments, video, television and a developing use of mask, role and narrative provided a very specific route away from the influence of minimal art.[55] Her first explicit appropriations of narrative emerged in *The Juniper Tree* (1976), and were developed through *Upside Down and Backwards* (1979), *Double Lunar Dogs* (1980), which drew on science-fiction, and *Volcano Saga* (1989), which incorporated Icelandic myth. An engagement with theatre convention and dramatic narrative is also evident in her work as a performer with the Wooster Group, first in *Nyatt School* (1978) and more recently in *Brace Up!* (1990).

Upside Down and Backwards begins with a recording of Jonas's own version of two Grimm Brothers' fairy tales, *The Frog Prince* and *The Boy Who Went Out to Learn Fear*. Yet the telling of the stories is disrupted, as *The Frog Prince* is presented in reverse order and the two stories are collaged together paragraph by paragraph:

> My stomach is full and I am tired, so carry me to your satin bed and we will lie together. The girl was afraid of the cold green frog but her father gave her angry looks, so, picking the frog up and holding him at arm's length, she went to her room and put him in a corner, but as she lay down he crawled over and threatened to tell her father if she did not take him to bed.
>
> In the dry and empty land there was a boy who had never known fear. Not the darkest night, the desert snakes, or the twisting winds. They wanted him to earn a living but he said that first he would like to learn fear. They didn't understand. One night they tried to frighten him in the old adobe bell tower, but he just got angry, so his father kicked him out of the house. 'No son of mine ...'[56]

Despite Jonas's intervention into the continuity of each story, the tone of her text is immediately recognisable. Although the collage confuses the content of the individual fables, the juxtaposition serves to heighten a sense of their common symmetry, rhythm and pattern. Ironically, though, while Jonas's reading of the stories reveals something of their formal nature, so it also serves to deny each narrative the possibility of establishing a single, unified and developing order.

Following the first two paragraphs Jonas enters the performance area. At the end of the sequence, she 'sits and plays a tune backwards on a music box, in which the paper roll has been reversed'.[57] The second part of the performance then begins, in which Jonas engages in a series of activities presented before three large paintings which dominate the stage. As she moves gradually from left to right, and so from one

painting to another, leaving a trail of objects behind her, a soundtrack
sets fragments of 1950s rock-and-roll against contemporary music, film
soundtrack and television. The soundtrack plays moments of *Let Me In*
by the Sensations; a fragment of a Cocteau film with the sound of frogs
croaking as a woman repeats '*Je t'aime*'; a tune from a music box, then
the same tune in reverse; the song *Yesyesyes* by the rock group The Res-
idents. Meanwhile Jonas translates her formal strategy of 'doubling'
into recurrent images of a double or doubles which shadow elements
drawn from the two fables. Manipulating her props, Jonas sets herself
against her double, a woman's head on a pole; she plays with a skeleton,
undressing it and dancing with it; she superimposes the image of a boy
painted on to glass over the skull. In the course of these activities
another double narrative is presented. Here, as Jonas papers the floor
with photocopies of landscape photographs, two soundtracks play
simultaneously in which she describes, in the first person, present tense,
activities, sights and impressions of two places. As she distributes the
photocopies, so she repeats the fragments of the tapes. The places echo
those from the fables, a woodland and a dry, arid place. The impression
they give, Jonas notes, is 'ominous' suggesting 'a loss of innocence'.[58]

Finally, moving backwards from left to right, Jonas reads from the
two intercut fairy-tales again, but this time they have been collaged
sentence by sentence:

> I am tired, so carry me to your bed and we will lie together. He was
> not afraid of the darkest nights, the desert snakes or the twisting
> winds, but she was, and so, picking him up, she threw him against the
> wall, and, as he fell, he turned into a man.[59]

Clearly, these fables are juxtaposed and their imagery reproduced and
echoed in such a way as to disrupt either narratives' ability to stabilise
the relationship between images and so circumscribe their meaning. Yet,
prefaced as they are by their sources within narrative, Jonas's images
refer back to narrative at the very moment at which they escape its
strictures.

This unravelling, in which the unifying function of narrative is disrupted through the presentation of explicitly narrative elements, has paradoxical consequences. While these images are clearly drawn from and
offered in relation to the fables, they are freed of the structures upon
which the stability of their meanings seemed to depend. The result is
neither a free flow of images nor a narrative continuity, but elements
torn between the two: between the narrative structures they recall and

the wide range of associations and references their freedom from narrative order makes apparent. Jonas extends this play on narrative by her extensive incorporation of quotations and appropriations. For the spectator, offered a ground and order that is put into question, the readings of these elements becomes difficult, continually under threat of displacement. Here, the centred perspective the narrative would promise is displaced, undermined by a free play of reference and allusion taken from the narrative and yet set against its closure.

In both *This is the story of a woman who ...* and *Upside Down and Backwards* narratives and narrative conventions are presented in such a way that their claim to authority is challenged. Yet this challenge to narrative is not simply a matter of competing or conflicting narratives, or even the successive displacement of one narrative by another. Here narratives are resisted or disrupted in such a way that the nature of their move toward unity and containment is made visible. Ironically, this work reveals the formal function and effect of the narrative voice by setting narrative elements against the move towards narrative closure, by deploying narrative voices against each other in such a way that the *event* of narration, the move toward containment, is frustrated and so made apparent.

A postmodern politics?

Read through such terms, the conflicts which *Route 1 & 9* and *The Constant State of Desire* so evidently foster can be seen as acutely and explicitly political extensions of this disruption of the move towards narrative closure. Like other Wooster Group performances, *Route 1 & 9* persistently disrupts not only the meaning of the stories it appropriates, such as Fadiman's lecture, *Our Town*, the Markham routines and, elsewhere, *The Crucible* or *Three Sisters*, but the stories it tells of these appropriations. Just as the authority of Fadiman's lecture is undermined, as is Wilder's claim to universality in *Our Town*, so the Wooster Group's own narrative claims come into question. Repeatedly, the Wooster Group implicate their own presentations in the processes they expose and critique. Indeed, such implication is inescapable where this critique is mounted against the claim to narrative voice and authority.

Like Rainer's late work, too, and consistently with this exposure of a struggle between narrative voices, these strategies bring the conflict between narrative possibilities on to a formal level. *Route 1 & 9* refuses to privilege the position of the viewer, resisting, through its self-conscious ironies and shifts of ground, any unself-conscious reading which would construct itself beyond the struggle between texts and perspectives. Indeed, this piece evidently effects a dangerous instability with regard to meaning in order that the viewer might contend with this struggle. The treatment of the blackface exemplifies this process. Subject to competing narratives, the blackface comes to occupy a space torn between meanings, a space which conflicting possibilities threaten to occupy in an impossible way. In reading the blackface, the viewer must enter into the struggle between voices and meanings, as a determination of what it *means* involves the giving of ascendency to one narrative over another. It may, then, be here that the most acutely uncomfortable aspects of *Route 1 & 9* lie as, if the re-enactment of the blackface is taken to be an act of degradation, the very collision between narratives begs the question of where the responsibility for that degradation actually lies.

Such a struggle between narrative claims is not a matter of articulating political meanings, but of making visible a politics of who speaks and who is spoken for. In this way, and far from reading the collision between texts as an attempt to shrug off responsibility for meaning, the paradoxical positions this work repeatedly strikes may be read as precipitating an 'event' with regard to meaning; the contesting of meaning, the struggle between narrative possibilities. By implicating themselves in this process of claim and counter-claim, the Wooster Group's strategies turn away from the question of *the meaning* and toward the *act* of making meaning.

In *The Constant State of Desire*, Finley, too, provokes such a struggle. Like the Wooster Group, her continual shifts of voice and narrative mode operate not simply on a thematic but a formal level, undercutting the position of the spectator and drawing her into a conflict between narratives and representations. So Finley's various narrative voices put each other into question, while her attack upon the 'sexuality of violence'[60] is made through an appropriation of languages whose rehearsal threatens to invite a reading through the very terms she would condemn.

In contrast to the Wooster Group, though, the space these conflicting narratives threaten to occupy is that marked out by Finley herself. At stake in *The Constant State of Desire* is a reading or construction of Finley as an active subject or her objectification and abuse through the terms she replays. In this context Finley's mode of performance gains a special significance. Rather than present a simple sequence of monologues, Finley shadows their presentation by her own steps in and out of a performance, her vacillations between formal and informal relationships with the audience. Here, Finley's concern to show that 'performance is hard to do', to trace out the *act* of performance, puts into question the claim of her various narratives to the ground she herself occupies. *The Constant State of Desire* not only offers differing voices and perspectives, threatening to block together conflicting narrative possibilities, but shadows this with the *event* of her telling, an event which is beyond the terms of any narrative. Through these means Finley moves to stave off a narrative closure, to place herself beyond the reach and so terms of the languages she uses and, in using, parodies.

Such a preoccupation with a performance's coming into being, with a shadowing of the performance by the act of performance, is evident too in the Wooster Group's work. Commenting on the incorporation of dances combining ballet exercises and flamenco at the end of *L.S.D.*, as four of the Wooster Group performers stand in for 'Donna Sierra and the Del Fuegos', a dance group who, it appears, have failed to turn up, LeCompte draws attention to just such a moment:

> To watch the dancer drop out to prepare for the next Raga was the most exciting thing for me – to watch that transformation. This dance was a kind of play on that. Kate Valk picks up these idiot ragas – there's nothing to them – but the whole thing is about the change of persona. From the preparation to the execution of the dance with such incredible aplomb. That's what dancing is about! It doesn't matter what you do, it's how you do it.[61]

Through specific devices, such as Willem Dafoe's dripping of glycerine into his eyes before the audience in order that he might 'cry' in *L.S.D.* or the handicapping of the blackface performers, as well as through the clash of performance styles itself, the Wooster Group's performances threaten to shadow and disrupt that which is being performed with the act of performance. Such strategies are concerned with those events which cannot be encompassed *within* narrative, that cannot be represented, and which shadow and qualify representation, that mark out or make visible the fact and limitation of representation. Indeed, in these respects, these performances attempt to qualify their engagement in their various discourses through a concern for 'figure', a concern for the event of the telling, of that aspect of narrative which discourse can neither encompass nor escape but would suppress.

Clearly, the Wooster Group and Karen Finley's performances are constructed towards a dangerous instability with regard to their meanings. Yet these presentations engage in a decidedly political resistance to narrative closure and, with this, a making visible of the nature and

consequences of the narrative act. The effect of such a resistance is not
to be found in a particular import or articulation of a point of view, but
occurs as a destabilising of that which is 'assumed', of that which would
appear to the audience as something which is already 'known'. Operating in this way, as a series of intrusions and disruptions, this performance also resists the attempt to divorce its 'meanings' or political
value from its immediate contexts. LeCompte's own notion of the political effect of the Wooster Group's work seems to echo this idea. Commenting on her interest in *The Crucible*, which was incorporated into
early versions of *L.S.D.*, she observes that:

> I felt we could do this play better than anyone in creation because of
> our particular distance. It's a distanced political play that takes its
> power from the situation in which it was written, not from the inter-
> nal relationships. That is so often the way in which our work is
> conceived.[62]

Such a description of the political value of certain kinds of formal
strategies clearly has a wider resonance. After Lyotard, and simply in
order to be consistent, one cannot confine such a notion of the 'political'
to that work which incorporates overtly social and political narratives and
images. In so far as the Wooster Group's and Karen Finley's performances effect a disruption of the 'meaningful', upsetting the hierarchies
and assumption that would define and stabilise the formal and thematic
parameters of their work, their strategies echo Kaprow's, Brecht's and
the Judson dancers' attacks on the stability of the 'object'. Although formally quite distinct from a quotation and subversion of 'texts', these
earlier presentations nevertheless intervened into reading, playing on
and problematising the viewer's desire for 'completion' and closure.
Although eschewing narrative, they similarly called into question the
authority of the 'work', just as they rendered uncertain the status and
meaning of that which the viewer encountered 'through' it. Such presentations may readily be set against Lyotard's understanding of the significance of aesthetic transgression, and the playing out of the resistance
to the 'illusion' of totalisation for which he calls. 'The price to pay for
such an illusion', Lyotard argues 'is terror', and he concludes that:

> the nineteenth and twentieth centuries have given us as much terror as
> we can take. We have paid a high enough price for the nostalgia of the
> whole and the one ... Let us wage a war on totality.[63]

In conclusion, then, and in something of the spirit of a resistance to closure, these ideas serve to turn attention back towards that work which has already been considered in this book, and which, although removed to one degree or another from a social and political 'content', nevertheless intrudes upon and disrupts the unself-conscious move toward closure.

Conclusion

Postmodernism and Performance

As it is taken here, the postmodern is not the property of a particular form or vocabulary. In so far as the postmodern in art may be identified with an unstable 'event' provoked by a questioning that casts doubt sharply upon even itself, then one characteristic of the postmodern would be its resistance to any simple circumscription of its means and forms. As a disruption of 'foundation' or a striving toward foundation, this postmodernism is best thought of as an *effect* of particular strategies played out in response to certain expectations. Indeed, the limitation of 'postmodern' means or the abstraction of predominant or defining 'post-modern' forms can only move against those instabilities which one might wish to identify as postmodern, so drawing the postmodern implicitly back towards foundation and the modern. It follows, then, that a description of 'postmodernism' must be given over to an account of postmodernism*s*, and so to an acknowledgement of the multiple means by which particular kinds of contingencies are revealed.

This view of diverse and multiple postmodernisms is one that lends itself to an address to those kinds of presentations and activities in the arts which corrupt conventional divisions and categories, or that are resistant to the very modes of looking and reading which they invite. For these reasons, the postmodernism debate can readily be used to pro-vide a framework of ideas through which to explore and test that reach-ing towards theatre which springs from interdisciplinary practices and sensibilities. Importantly, too, this idea of the 'postmodern event' allows an exploration of connections between very obviously divergent

144

kinds of work which meet in a making visible of the unsteady agreements and circumstances upon which the work of art and its meanings depend.

In looking towards these points of contact between differing forms, practices and ideas, however, this study does not attempt to observe connections between 'postmodernism' and 'performance' in any impartial way. In this book, the postmodern is overtly defined and 'limited' in order to allow a particular address to take place. It follows that, to be consistent, a project which looks towards the production of such 'postmodern' instabilities must also invite a questioning of its own terms and limits. One might challenge, then, the ways in which the exclusions this book makes serve to construct a predominant view, moving implicitly towards a circumscription of ideas, means and forms. In looking towards performance which is touched on but not considered in detail here, one might both use and challenge the move towards categories this study effects. Thus Laurie Anderson's performance, *United States*, of 1983, might be read as resisting a consideration either through a disruption of narrative, after the Wooster Group, or as an attack on the efficacy of the sign, after Richard Foreman. Yet Anderson's appropriations and displacements of popular imagery and her telling of paradoxical stories around these images might be considered by setting these two readings against each other, using and challenging the distinctions between them.

Indeed, the resistance to category that underlies this notion of the postmodern might be set against the implicit privileging, here, of performance as a 'primary postmodern mode'. If the postmodern occurs as a disruption of discourse and representation, then it cannot be associated in any exclusive way with a particular form or mode. If the 'postmodern event' occurs as a breaking away, a disruption of what is 'given', then 'its' forms cannot usefully be pinned down in any final or categorical way. In this case, where the postmodern is represented in one way, where 'its' means are defined, then the 'postmodern event' will come into play at the very moment this limitation, and so the move toward closure, is disrupted. Such definitions cannot arrive at the postmodern, but can only set out a ground which might be challenged.

To 'use' the postmodern, though, and so to deliberately 'limit' it, might not be, quite, to define it. Limiting the postmodern might be more like a local activity, one that tacitly acknowledges its own parameters as much as it strives to confine the postmodernism debate. Rather than seek to *totalise* and so *possess* the term, to hold it within a particular categorical and formal definition, such a limitation might look towards an interrogation of its own terms and assumptions. This invitation is more consistent with the 'postmodern' as it is taken here than could be any particular definition of postmodern forms or features, as it is an invitation that calls for a resistance to a drawing of the postmodern back towards the foundation it would disrupt.

Notes

Notes to the Introduction

1. G. Vattimo, *The End of Modernity* (Oxford, 1988) p. 2.
2. See, for example, J. B. Alter, 'A Critical Analysis of Suzanne K. Langer's Dance Theory', *Dance Research Annual*, vol. XVI (1987) pp. 110–19; and M. Sheets-Johnstone, 'On the Nature of Theories of Dance', *CORD Dance Research Annual*, vol. X (1979) pp. 3–29.

Notes to Chapter 1

1. Although the development of 'postmodern' design can be traced back, at least, to the work of Robert Venturi in the early 1960s (see R. Venturi, *Complexity and Contradiction in Architecture* (New York, 1966), Portoghesi argues that modern design had become untenable by 1968. In *What is Post-modernism?*, 2nd edn (London, 1987) Charles Jencks, tongue-in-cheek, dates the 'Death of Modernism/Rise of Post-modernism' from the dynamiting of the Pruitt-Igoe housing complex in St Louis in 1972.
2. P. Portoghesi, *Postmodern: The Architecture of Postindustrial Society* (New York, 1982) p. 11.
3. Ibid., p. 12.
4. Ibid., p. 7.
5. Ibid.
6. U. Conrads, *Programmes and Manifestos on Twentieth Century Architecture* (London, 1970) p. 74.
7. C. Jencks, *Post-modernism: The New Classicism in Art and Architecture* (London, 1987) p. 330.
8. H. Klotz, *The History of Postmodern Architecture* (London, 1988) p. 421.

9. See, particularly, C. Jencks, *What is Post-modernism?*, 2nd edn (London, 1987) and *Post-modernism: The New Classicism in Art and Architecture* (London, 1987).
10. Jencks, *Post-modernism*, p. 268.
11. Ibid., p. 271.
12. Ibid., p. 272.
13. Ibid.
14. Ibid.
15. Ibid., p. 338.
16. Ibid., p. 345.
17. Ibid., p. 340.
18. Ibid., p. 345.
19. Conrads, *Programmes and Manifestos*, p. 95.
20. See Klotz, *History of Postmodern Architecture*, p. 20.
21. Conrads, *Programmes and Manifestos*, p. 25.
22. Le Corbusier, *Towards a New Architecture* (London, 1927) p. 20.
23. L. Hutcheon, *A Poetics of Postmodernism* (London, 1988) p. 3.
24. Ibid., p. 92.
25. Ibid., p. 108.
26. Ibid., p. 107.
27. J. Kalb, 'Ping Chong: From *Lazarus* to *Anna into Nightlight*', *Theater*, vol. XIV, no. 2 (1983) pp. 68–75, esp. p. 68.
28. N. Carrol, 'A Select View of Earthlings: Ping Chong', *Drama Review*, vol. XXVII, no. 1 (1983) pp. 72–81.
29. See, for example, H. Papaport, ' "Can You Say Hello?": Laurie Anderson's *United States*', *Theatre Journal*, vol. XXXVIII, no. 3 (1986) pp. 339–54.
30. See, for example, W. W. Demastes, 'Spalding Gray's *Swimming to Cambodia* and the Evolution of an Ironic Presence', *Theatre Journal*, vol. XXXXI, no. 1 (1989) pp. 75–94.
31. See N. Kaye, 'Richard Schechner: Theory and Practice of the Indeterminate Theatre', *New Theatre Quarterly*, vol. V, no. 20 (1989) pp. 348–60.
32. Hutcheon, *Poetics of Postmodernism*, p. 11.
33. J. Derrida, *Of Grammatology* (London, 1976) p. 7.
34. For Derrida's discussion of Saussure and structural linguistics see, particularly, *Of Grammatology*, pp. 27–73.
35. See, for example, H. Foster, 'Wild Signs: the Breakup of the Sign in '70s Art', in J. Tagg (ed.), *The Cultural Politics of Postmodernism* (New York, 1989).
36. J. Baudrillard, *The Ecstasy of Communication* (New York, 1987) p. 11.

37. J. F. Lyotard, *The Postmodern Condition: A Report on Knowledge* (Manchester, 1984) p. xxvii.

38. Ibid., p. xxiv.

39. B. Readings, *Introducing Lyotard: Art and Politics* (London, 1991) p. 69.

40. Ibid., p. 79.

41. See O. Paz, *Children of the Mire* (Harvard, Mass., 1974), Ch. 1: 'A Tradition Against Itself'.

42. Lyotard, *Postmodern Condition*, p. 79.

43. Readings, *Introducing Lyotard*, p. 74.

44. Baudrillard, *Ecstasy of Communication*, p. 11.

45. See T. Docherty, *After Theory: Post-modernism/Post-Marxism* (London, 1990). Docherty uses the term 'backward glance' to indicate the construction of a legitimating historical perspective.

46. U. Eco, *Reflections on 'The Name of the Rose'* (London, 1985) p. 67.

47. S. Lash, *Sociology of Postmodernism* (London, 1990) p. 157.

48. Ibid., p. 173.

49. See, particularly, M. Fried, 'Art and Objecthood', in G. Battcock (ed.), *Minimal Art: A Critical Anthology* (New York, 1968).

Notes to Chapter 2

1. See, for example, S. Banes, *Democracy's Body: Judson Dance Theater, 1962–1964* (Ann Arbor, Mich., 1983); and R. Goldberg, *Performance Art* (London, 1988) pp. 141–3.

2. C. Greenberg, ' "American-type" Painting', in C. Greenberg, *Art and Culture: Critical Essays* (Boston, Mass., 1965) p. 210.

3. C. Greenberg, 'After Abstract Expressionism', *Art International*, vol. VI, no. 8 (1962) pp. 26–30, esp. p. 30.

4. Greenberg, ' "American-type" Painting', p. 209.

5. Ibid., p. 210.

6. C. Greenberg, 'After Abstract Expressionism', *Art International*, vol. VI, no. 8 (1962) pp. 26–30, esp. p. 30.

7. C. Greenberg, 'Modernist Painting', *Art and Literature*, vol. 4 (1965) pp. 193–201, esp. p. 194.

8. Ibid., p. 193.

9. Ibid., p. 195.

10. C. Greenberg, 'Avant-garde and Kitsch', in Greenberg, *Art and Culture*, pp. 5–6.

11. Greenberg, 'Modernist Painting', p. 200.
12. V. Acconci, *Recorded documentation by Vito Acconci of the exhibition and commission for San Diego State University*, April–May 1982 (audio cassette) (San Diego, Cal., 1982).
13. M. Fried, 'Art and Objecthood', in G. Battcock (ed.), *Minimal Art: A Critical Anthology* (New York, 1968) p. 125.
14. Ibid., p. 145.
15. Ibid., p. 135.
16. Ibid., p. 141.
17. Ibid., p. 142.
18. L. Alloway, 'Rauschenberg's Development', in Smithsonian Institute, *Robert Rauschenberg* (Washington, D.C., 1976) p. 3.
19. Ibid., p. 5.
20. Greenberg, 'After Abstract Expressionism', p. 26.
21. M. Crichton, *Jasper Johns* (London, 1977) p. 40.
22. A. Kaprow, *Assemblages, Environments and Happenings* (New York, 1966) p. 159.
23. Ibid., p. 165.
24. Ibid., p. 169.
25. First emerging in New York in 1961 under the organisation of gallery owner George Maciunas, 'Fluxus' became a name under which a continually growing and changing number of American and European artists presented concerts and published books and proposals. Characterised above all by an eclecticism and informality, Fluxus might be best described as a manner of work or a certain kind of sensibility. In describing Fluxus 'art-amusement' as 'the fusion of Spike Jones, Vaudeville, gag, children's games and Duchamp', Maciunas went some way toward identifying the spirit of their activities.
26. The Reuben Gallery, *George Brecht: toward Events*, announcement of exhibition (New York, 1959).
27. C. Oldenburg, *Store Days* (New York, 1967) p. 200.
28. A script and documentation of *18 Happenings in 6 Parts*, among a range of other early presentations, is published in M. Kirby, *Happenings* (New York, 1965).
29. See, for example, J. Cage, 'An Interview', *Tulane Drama Review*, vol. x, no. 2 (1965) pp. 50–72.
30. See Fried, 'Art and Objecthood', p. 124. Fried notes his disagreement here with his earlier view of modernism set out in his article 'Three American Painters'.
31. Fried, 'Art and Objecthood', pp. 123–4.

32. See, particularly, D. M. Levin, 'Postmodernism in Dance: Dance, Discourse, Democracy', in H. J. Silverman (ed.), *Postmodernism – Philosophy and the Arts* (London, 1990). Levin draws on Greenberg and Fried to argue that the modernist work is one which reveals, reflects upon and displaces those conditions which have served to define the work of art under a particular set of (contingent) historical conditions. Levin goes on to argue that, in its deconstruction of the modern, the modernist work comprises a first phase of postmodernism, and one that gives way to the specifically postmodernist. Levin defines postmodernism in art in terms of an historical break from the modern and a subsequent and general chronological development.

33. Fried, 'Art and Objecthood', p. 123.

34. A. Kaprow, 'Self-Service: a Happening', *Drama Review*, vol. XII, no. 3 (1968) pp. 160–4, esp. pp. 161–4.

35. R. Kostalanetz, *The Theatre of Mixed Means* (New York, 1968) p. 112.

36. Kaprow, *Assemblages, Environments and Happenings*, p. 193.

37. A. Kaprow, 'Education of the Un-artist, Part Two', *Art News*, vol. LXXI, no. 3 (1972) pp. 34–9, 62, esp. p. 35.

38. A. Kaprow and R. Schechner, 'Extensions in Time and Space', *Drama Review*, vol. XII, no. 2 (1968) pp. 153–9, esp. p. 154.

39. Ibid., p. 153.

40. Kaprow, 'Self-Service: a Happening', pp. 160–4.

41. Ibid., p. 161.

42. Kaprow and Schechner, 'Extensions in Time and Space', p. 154.

43. Ibid.

44. A. Kaprow, 'The Happenings are Dead: Long Live the Happenings', *Artforum*, vol. IV, no. 7 (1966) pp. 36–9, esp. p. 39.

45. Ibid.

46. *Three Aqueous Events* was originally published in George Brecht's *Water Yam* (Fluxus: New York, 1962). According to Brecht, a first edition of approximately 60 cards was expanded to an edition of 105 or 110 in 1964 or 1965. Other sources for Brecht 'event-scores' include H. Ruhe (ed.), *Fluxus: the most radical and experimental art movement of the sixties* (Amsterdam, 1979); and *Film Culture*, vol. 43 (1966).

47. H. Martin, 'An Interview with George Brecht by Henry Martin', in H. Martin, *An Introduction to George Brecht's Book of the Tumbler on Fire* (Milan, 1978) p. 84.

48. See, for example, I. Lebeer, 'An Interview with George Brecht by

Irmilene Lebeer', in Martin, *An Introduction to George Brecht's Book*, p. 87.

49. From my own correspondence with the artist, December 1983.
50. Martin, *An Introduction to George Brecht's Book*, pp. 27–8.
51. G. Brecht and A. Kaprow, 'Excerpts from a discussion between George Brecht and Allan Kaprow entitled: "Happening and Events" ', in H. Sohm (ed.), *Happenings and Fluxus* (Cologne, 1971) pages unnumbered.
52. Martin, *An Introduction to George Brecht's Book*, p. 10.
53. See M. Kirby, *Happenings* (New York, 1965) p. 21.
54. Lebeer, 'Interview with George Brecht'.
55. A. Kaprow, 'Non-theatrical Performance', *Artforum*, vol. XIV, no. 9 (1976) pp. 45–51, esp. pp. 49–50.
56. Martin, *An Introduction to George Brecht's Book*, pp. 10–11.
57. J. Van der Marck, 'George Brecht: an Art of Multiple Implications', *Art in America*, vol. LXII, no. 4 (1974) pp. 48–57, esp. p. 51.
58. Martin, 'An Interview with George Brecht by Henry Martin', pp. 77–8.
59. Ibid., p. 77.
60. M. Alocco and B. Vautier, 'A Conversation About Something Else: an Interview with George Brecht by Marcel Alocco and Ben Vautier', in Martin, *An Introduction to George Brecht's Book*, pp. 69–70.
61. M. Nyman, 'An Interview with George Brecht by Michael Nyman', in Martin, *An Introduction to George Brecht's Book*, p. 120.

Notes to Chapter 3

1. See, particularly, T. Shank, *American Alternative Theatre* (London, 1982). Shank groups Wilson and Kirby together on the grounds that 'form or structure' are 'the predominant content of their work' (p. 123). See also R. Schechner, 'The Decline and Fall of the (American) Avant-garde', in R. Schechner, *The End of Humanism* (New York, 1982). Schechner argues that work by Foreman, Wilson and others in the 1970s heralded a 'formalist deep freeze ... great work was done, but it was cut off; it did not manifest significant content' (p. 18).
2. N. Kaye and M. Kirby, unpublished interview, New York, April 1990.
3. M. Feingold, 'An Interview with Richard Foreman', *Theatre*, vol. VII, no. 1 (1975) pp. 5–29, esp. p. 25.

4. Ibid., p. 10.

5. N. Kaye, 'Bouncing Back the Impulse: an Interview with Richard Foreman', *Performance*, vol. 61 (1990) pp. 31–42, esp. p. 32.

6. S. Brecht, *The Theatre of Visions* (Frankfurt am Main, 1978) pp. 21–2.

7. Ibid., p. 26.

8. Ibid., p. 28.

9. Ibid., p. 45.

10. R. Foreman, 'How to Write a Play', in R. Foreman, *Reverberation Machines: The Later Plays and Essays* (New York, 1985) p. 222.

11. M. Kirby, 'Structural Analysis/Structural Theory', *Drama Review*, vol. XX, no. 4 (1976) pp. 51–68, esp. p. 53.

12. R. Foreman, *Ontological-Hysteric Manifesto I*, in K. Davy (ed.), *Richard Foreman: Plays and Manifestos* (New York, 1976) p. 69.

13. R. Foreman, *Pandering to the Masses: A Misrepresentation*, in B. Marranca (ed.), *The Theatre of Images* (New York, 1977) pp. 15–36.

14. Ibid., p. 26.

15. Ibid., p. 16.

16. Ibid.

17. Ibid.

18. See K. Davy, 'Review: Foreman's Pandering', *Drama Review*, vol. XIX, no. 1 (1975) pp. 116–17, esp. p. 117.

19. Marranca (ed.), *The Theatre of Images*, p. 12.

20. R. Foreman, 'How Truth . . . Leaps (Stumbles) Across Stage', in Foreman, *Reverberation Machines*, p. 198.

21. R. Foreman, 'How I Write My (Self:Plays)', *Drama Review*, vol. XXI, no. 4 (1977) pp. 5–24, esp. p. 21.

22. Foreman, *Ontological-Hysteric Manifesto I*, p. 76.

23. Foreman, 'How I Write My (Self:Plays)', p. 13.

24. Foreman, 'How Truth . . . Leaps (Stumbles) Across Stage', p. 198.

25. R. Foreman, *Ontological-Hysteric: Manifesto II*, in Davy (ed.), *Richard Foreman: Plays and Manifestos*, p. 137.

26. Ibid., p. 145.

27. Foreman, 'How to Write a Play', p. 224.

28. As well as being instrumental to innovations in dance (see Chapter 5), chance method was of particular importance to Fluxus work and many early Happenings. Several of George Brecht's 'event-scores' explicitly draw on Cage's methods.

29. Foreman, *Ontological-Hysteric Manifesto I*, p. 68.

30. R. Foreman, '14 Things I Tell Myself', in Foreman, *Reverberation Machines*, p. 215.

31. Foreman, 'How Truth ... Leaps (Stumbles) Across Stage', p. 199.
32. K. Davy, 'Foreman's *Vertical Mobility* and *PAIN(T)*', *Drama Review*, vol. XVIII, no. 2 (1974) pp. 26–37, esp. p. 34.
33. Ibid., p. 35.
34. Kaye, 'Bouncing Back the Impulse', p. 34.
35. Foreman, *Ontological-Hysteric Manifesto I*, p. 68.
36. K. Davy, 'Kate Manheim on Foreman's Rhoda', *Drama Review*, vol. XX, no. 3 (1976) pp. 37–50, esp. p. 43.
37. Ibid.
38. Ibid.
39. Foreman, *Ontological-Hysteric Manifesto I*, p. 70.
40. Foreman, *Ontological-Hysteric: Manifesto II*, p. 143.
41. Kaye, 'Bouncing Back the Impulse', p. 39.
42. Foreman, 'How to Write a Play', p. 229.
43. Kaye and Kirby, unpublished interview.
44. Ibid.
45. M. Kirby, *First Signs of Decadence* (Schulenburg, 1986) p. xiii.
46. Ibid., p. vi.
47. Ibid., p. xiii.
48. Kaye and Kirby, unpublished interview.
49. Kirby, *First Signs of Decadence*, p. x.
50. Ibid, p. viii.
51. Kaye and Kirby, unpublished interview.
52. Kirby, *First Signs of Decadence*, p. 19.
53. Ibid., p. 24.
54. Ibid., p. 15.
55. Ibid., p. 30.
56. Ibid., p. xi.
57. Kaye and Kirby, unpublished interview.
58. Kirby, *First Signs of Decadence*, p. 13.
59. Ibid., p. 19.
60. Ibid., p. 34.
61. Ibid., p. 23.
62. Brecht, *Theatre of Visions*, pp. 54–5.
63. Ibid., p. 55.
64. L. Shyer, *Robert Wilson and his Collaborators* (New York, 1989) p. 6.
65. Brecht, *Theatre of Visions*, p. 115.
66. O. Trilling, 'Robert Wilson's *Ka Mountain*', *Drama Review*, vol. XVII, no. 2 (1973) pp. 33–47, esp. p. 44.
67. Shyer, *Robert Wilson*, p. 7.
68. Brecht, *Theatre of Visions*, p. 55.

69. Trilling, 'Robert Wilson's *Ka Mountain*', p. 44.
70. Shyer, *Robert Wilson*, pp. 6–7.
71. Brecht, *Theatre of Visions*, p. 55.
72. Ibid.
73. Ibid., pp. 56–7.
74. Ibid., p. 58.
75. Ibid., p. 210.
76. Ibid., p. 390.
77. Ibid., p. 172.
78. Wilson's early work was performed by a changing company of largely untrained performers. Wilson used the idiosyncratic qualities of his performers in the manner of 'found' elements in the construction of his collages. See, in particular, Shyer, *Robert Wilson*; and B. Simmer, 'Sue Sheehy', *Drama Review*, vol. XX, no. 1 (1976) pp. 67–74.
79. Brecht, *Theatre of Visions*, p. 420.
80. Ibid., p. 419.
81. J. Donker, *President of Paradise: A traveller's account of Robert Wilson's 'the CIVIL warS'* (Amsterdam, 1985) pp. 23–4.
82. In particular, the King of Spain in *The King of Spain* (1969), Sigmund Freud in *The Life and Times of Sigmund Freud* (1970), Joseph Stalin in *The Life and Times of Joseph Stalin* (1973), Queen Victoria in *A Letter for Queen Victoria* (1974), Einstein in *Einstein on the Beach* (1976), Thomas Edison in *Edison* (1979), Rudolph Hess in *Death, Destruction and Detroit* (1979) and Abraham Lincoln in *the CIVIL warS* (1984).
83. For example, *A Letter for Queen Victoria* (1974) and *The Golden Windows* (1982).
84. Shyer, *Robert Wilson*, p. 80.
85. Brecht, *Theatre of Visions*, p. 274.
86. Ibid., p. 277.
87. Shyer, *Robert Wilson*, p. 216.
88. Donker, *President of Paradise*, p. 117.
89. Brecht, *Theatre of Visions*, p. 420.
90. Ibid., p. 425.
91. Foreman, '14 Things I Tell Myself', p. 213.

Notes to Chapter 4

1. L. Horst and C. Russell, *Modern Dance Forms* (San Francisco, 1961) p. 16.

2. See, for example, M. B. Siegel, 'Modern Dance at Bennington: Sorting It All Out', *Dance Research Journal*, vol. XIX, no. 1 (1987) pp. 3–9.
3. Ibid.
4 J. H. Mazo, *Prime Movers* (London, 1977) p. 121.
5. Ibid., p. 123.
6. Ibid., p. 184.
7. S. L. Foster, *Reading Dancing: Bodies and Subjects in Contemporary American Dance* (Berkeley, Cal., 1986) p. 150.
8. Horst and Russell, *Modern Dance Forms*, p. 23.
9. Ibid., p. 24.
10. Ibid.
11. See S. Banes, *Democracy's Body: Judson Dance Theater, 1962–1964* (Ann Arbor, Mich., 1983) p. 3.
12. Ibid., p. 3.
13. Ibid., p. xviii.
14. Ibid.
15. S. Banes, *Terpsichore in Sneakers: Post-modern Dance*, 2nd edn (Middletown, Conn., 1987) p. xiv.
16. See J. Hendricks (ed.), *Fluxus Etc.: The Gilbert and Lila Silverman Collection* (Bloomfield Hills, Mich., 1981) Part 3, a chronology of Fluxus performance.
17. See Banes, *Democracy's Body*, pp. 131–2.
18. M. Fried, 'Art and Objecthood', in G. Battcock (ed.), *Minimal Art: A Critical Anthology* (New York, 1968) p. 140.
19. Ibid.
20. Foster, *Reading Dancing*, p. xiv.
21. Ibid., p. xvi.
22. C. Sachs, *World History of the Dance* (New York, 1937) p. 447.
23. J. Martin, *Introduction to the Dance* (New York, 1939) p. 224.
24. Ibid., p. 32.
25. Horst and Russell, *Modern Dance Forms*, pp. 13–14.
26. Ibid., p. 13.
27. Foster, *Reading Dancing*, p. xvi.
28. S. K. Langer, *Feeling and Form: A Theory of Art* (London, 1953) p. 23.
29. Ibid., p. 39.
30. Ibid.
31. Ibid., p. 31.
32. Ibid., p. 67.
33. Ibid., p. 45.

34. Ibid., p. 46.
35. Ibid., p. 45.
36. Ibid., p. 84.
37. Ibid., p. 71.
38. Ibid., pp. 71–2.
39. Ibid., p. 72.
40. Ibid.
41. Ibid., p. 73.
42. Ibid., p. 178.
43. Ibid., p. 175.
44. Ibid., p. 205.
45. Ibid., p. 184.
46. Ibid., p. 59.
47. J. Martin, *The Modern Dance* (New York, 1933) p. 84.
48. Ibid., p. 4.
49. Ibid., p. 6.
50. Ibid.
51. Ibid., pp. 7–8.
52. Ibid., p. 15.
53. Ibid., p. 31.
54. Ibid.
55. Ibid., p. 33.
56. Ibid., p. 35.
57. Ibid., p. 91.
58. Ibid., p. 90.
59. Ibid., p. 85.
60. Ibid., p. 86.
61. Ibid., p. 47.
62. Langer, *Feeling and Form*, p. 175.
63. Horst and Russell, *Modern Dance Forms*, p. 117.
64. Ibid., pp. 117–18.

Notes to Chapter 5

1. S. Banes, *Democracy's Body: Judson Dance Theater, 1962–1964* (Ann Arbor, Mich., 1983) p. 1.
2. Ibid., p. 2.
3. Ibid., p. 7.
4. Ibid., p. 39.
5. Ibid., p. 11.

6. Ibid., p. 44.
7. Ibid., p. 65.
8. Ibid., p. 58.
9. N. Kaye, unpublished interview with John Cage, London, May 1985.
10. J. Cage, 'Experimental Music', in J. Cage, *Silence: Lectures and Writings* (London, 1968) p. 8.
11. J. Cage, 'Lecture on Nothing', in Cage, *Silence*, p. 111.
12. J. Cage and D. Charles, *For the Birds* (London, 1981) p. 153.
13. Ibid., p. 180.
14. Ibid., p. 201.
15. Ibid., p. 52.
16. Kaye, unpublished interview.
17. J. Cage, 'To Describe the Process of Composition Used in *Music of Changes* and *Imaginary Landscape No. 4*', in Cage, *Silence*, p. 58.
18. Banes, *Democracy's Body*, p. 43.
19. Ibid., p. 47.
20. Ibid.
21. Ibid., pp. 59–60.
22. Ibid., p. 60.
23. Ibid., p. 7.
24. Ibid., p. 8.
25. Ibid., pp. 8–9.
26. S. Forti, *Handbook in Motion* (New York, 1974) p. 36.
27. Ibid., p. 44.
28. R. Morris, 'Notes on Dance', *Tulane Drama Review*, vol. X, no. 2 (1965) pp. 179–86, esp. p. 179.
29. A. Livet (ed.), *Contemporary Dance* (New York, 1978) p. 45.
30. Kaye, unpublished interview.
31. Banes, *Democracy's Body*, pp. 87, 90–1.
32. Ibid., p. 78.
33. Ibid., p. 86.
34. Y. Rainer, *Work, 1961–73* (Nova Scotia and New York, 1974) pp. 67–8.
35. Ibid., p. 66.
36. Ibid., p. 67.
37. Ibid.
38. Ibid., p. 68.
39. Foster, *Reading Dancing*, p. 175.
40. Ibid., p. 176.
41. Banes, *Terpsichore in Sneakers*, p. 44.

42. Rainer, *Work, 1961–73*, p. 67.
43. Ibid.
44. Banes, *Terpsichore in Sneakers*, p. 61.
45. S. Paxton, score and notes for *Satisfyin Lover*, in Banes, *Terpsichore in Sneakers*, p. 71.
46. Banes, *Democracy's Body*, p. 60.
47. L. Childs, 'Lucinda Childs: a Portfolio', *Artforum*, vol. 11 (1973) pp. 50–7, esp. p. 50.
48. Ibid.
49. L. Childs, 'Notes: '64–'74', *Drama Review*, vol. XIX, no. 1 (1975) pp. 33–6, esp. p. 33.
50. Ibid.
51. Childs, 'Lucinda Childs', p. 56.
52. Ibid., p. 55.
53. Childs, 'Notes: '64–'74', p. 34.
54. Ibid.
55. Ibid., pp. 34–5.
56. Livet, *Contemporary Dance*, p. 44.
57. E. Stefano, 'Moving Structures', *Art and Artists*, vol. VII, no. 10 (1974) pp. 16–25, esp. p. 17.
58. D. Jowitt, *Dance Beat: Selected Views and Reviews* (New York, 1977) p. 117.
59. T. Brown, 'Three Pieces', *Drama Review*, vol. XIX, no. 1 (1975) pp. 26–32, esp. p. 29.
60. Ibid.
61. Ibid.
62. Stefano, 'Moving Structures', p. 2 0.
63. R. Morris, 'Some Notes on the Phenomenology of Making', *Artforum*, vol. VIII, no. 6 (1970) pp. 62–4, esp. p. 63.
64. See, for example, M. Compton and D. Sylvester, *Robert Morris* (London, 1977) pp. 114–17.
65. Rainer, *Work, 1961–73*, p. 125.
66. Ibid., p. 130.
67. Ibid., p. 131.

Notes to Chapter 6

1. T. Wilder, *Our Town, The Skin of Our Teeth, The Matchmaker* (London, 1987) p. 7.

2. W. Coco, 'Review: *Route 1 & 9*', *Theatre Journal*, vol. XXXIV, no. 2 (1982) pp. 249–52, esp. p. 250.
3. D. Savran, *Breaking the Rules: The Wooster Group* (New York, 1988) p. 15.
4. Ibid., p. 21.
5. Ibid., p. 22.
6. Ibid., p. 30.
7. Ibid., p. 14.
8. Wilder, *Our Town*, p. 76.
9. Ibid.
10. Ibid., p. 11.
11. R. J. Burbank, *Thornton Wilder*, 2nd edn (New York, 1978) p. 72.
12. Ibid.
13. Wilder, *Our Town*, p. 89.
14. Savran, *Breaking the Rules*, p. 25.
15. Ibid., p. 27.
16. Coco, 'Review: *Route 1 & 9*', p. 251.
17. Savran, *Breaking the Rules*, p. 36.
18. Ibid., p. 43.
19. Ibid., p. 53.
20. Ibid., p. 31.
21. Ibid., p. 44.
22. According to Elizabeth LeCompte and Ron Vawter, the tape was developed before *Route 1 & 9* and derived from an interest in the nature of performance in pornographic film and the desire to make something 'private and possibly obscene'. See Savran, *Breaking the Rules*, pp. 41–5.
23. L. Champagne, 'Always Starting Anew: Elizabeth LeCompte', *Drama Review*, vol. XXV, no. 3 (1981) pp. 19–28, p. 25.
24. Savran, *Breaking the Rules*, p. 34.
25. Champagne, 'Always Starting Anew', p. 25.
26. See Savran, *Breaking the Rules*, pp. 26–33. The history and use of the blackface is widely charted. See, in particular, B. Ostendorf, *Black Literature in White America* (Totowa, N.J., 1982) ch. 3.
27. See Savran, *Breaking the Rules*, p. 10. Savran reports that an NYSCA memo concluded that '*Route 1 & 9* constituted in its blackface sequences harsh and caricatured portrayals of a racial minority'.
28. Champagne, 'Always Starting Anew', p. 36.
29. See, for example, D. Savran, 'The Wooster Group, Arthur Miller and *The Crucible*', *Drama Review*, vol. XXIX, no. 2 (1985) pp. 99–109.

30. Savran, *Breaking the Rules*, pp. 53–4.
31. See, for example, E. Fuchs, 'Staging the Obscene Body', *Drama Review*, vol. XXXIII, no. 1 (1989) pp. 33–58.
32. See, particularly, C. Schuler, 'Spectator Response and Comprehension: the Problem of Karen Finley's *The Constant State of Desire*', *Drama Review*, vol. XXXIV, no. 1 (1990) pp. 152–8.
33. Karen Finley's *The Constant State of Desire* has been published in three forms, reflecting the changing nature of the piece in performance. This discussion draws principally on the later publication in Finley's *Shock Treatment* (San Francisco, 1990), with some reference to her earlier publication of 'The Constant State of Desire' in *Drama Review*, vol. XXXII, no. 1 (1988) pp. 139–51. The earlier text includes stage-directions. Another version of the text is published in L. Champagne, *Out from Under: Texts by Women Performance Artists* (New York, 1990).
34. Finley, *Shock Treatment*, p. 3.
35. Ibid., p. 5.
36. Finley, 'The Constant State of Desire', p. 140.
37. Finley, *Shock Treatment*, p. 9.
38. Finley, 'The Constant State of Desire', p. 142.
39. Finley, *Shock Treatment*, pp. 9–10.
40. Ibid., p. 15.
41. Ibid.
42. Ibid., pp. 20–1.
43. J. Dolan, *The Feminist Spectator as Critic* (Ann Arbor, Mich., 1988) p. 67.
44. See, for example, M. Robinson, 'Performance Strategies: Interviews with Ishmael Houston-Jones, John Kelly, Karen Finley, Richard Elovich', *Performing Arts Journal*, vol. X, no. 3 (1987) pp. 31–56.
45. R. Schechner, 'Karen Finley: a Constant State of Becoming', *Drama Review*, vol. XXXII, no. 1 (1988) pp. 152–8, esp. p. 155.
46. Robinson, 'Performance Strategies', p. 44.
47. Y. Rainer, *Work, 1961–73* (Nova Scotia and New York, 1974) p. 251.
48. Ibid.
49. Ibid., p. 253.
50. Ibid., p. 257.
51. Ibid., p. 263.
52. P. Hulton, 'Fiction, Character and Narration: Yvonne Rainer', *Dartington Theatre Papers*, 2nd series, no. 7 (Dartington Hall, Devon, 1978), pp. 5–6.

53. Rainer, *Work, 1961–73*, p. 271.
54. Hulton, 'Fiction, Character and Narration', p. 12.
55. See N. Kaye, 'Mask, Role and Narrative: an Interview with Joan Jonas', *Performance*, vols 65–6 (1992) pp. 49–60.
56. J. Jonas, *Scripts and Descriptions* (Berkeley, Cal., 1983) p. 99.
57. Ibid.
58. Ibid., p. 103.
59. Ibid., p. 107.
60. Schechner, 'Karen Finley', p. 153.
61. A. Aronson, 'The Wooster Group's *L.S.D. (... Just the High Points ...)*', *Drama Review*, vol. XXIX, no. 2 (1985) pp. 65–77, esp. p. 73.
62. Ibid., p. 71.
63. J. F. Lyotard, *The Postmodern Condition: A Report on Knowledge* (Manchester, 1984) pp. 51–2.

Select Bibliography

From postmodern style to performance

Apignanesi, L., (ed.), *Postmodernism* (London, 1989).

Baudrillard, J., *Simulations* (New York, 1983).

——, *The Ecstasy of Communication* (New York, 1987).

——, *Cool Memories* (Paris, 1987).

——, *America* (London, 1989)

Benjamin, A., (ed.), *The Problems of Modernity: Adorno and Benjamin* (London, 1989).

Benjamin, W., *Illuminations* (London, 1968).

Birringer, J., *Theatre, Theory, Postmodernism* (Bloomington and Indianapolis, 1991).

Blau, H., *Blooded Thought* (New York, 1982).

——, *The Eye of Prey: Subversions of the Postmodern* (Bloomington and Indianapolis, 1987).

——, *The Audience* (Baltimore, Md, 1990).

Bradbury, M., and McFarlane, J. (eds), *Modernism: 1890–1930* (London, 1976).

Burgin, V., *The End of Art Theory: Criticism and Postmodernity* (London, 1986).

Butler, C., *After the Wake: An Essay on the Contemporary Avant-garde* (Oxford, 1980).

Calinescu, M., *Five Faces of Modernity: Modernism, Avant-garde, Decadence Kitsch, Postmodernism* (London, 1987).

Calinescu, M., and Fokkema, D. (eds), *Exploring Postmodernism* (Amsterdam and Philadelphia, 1990).

Carroll, D., *Paraesthetics: Foucault, Lyotard, Derrida* (London, 1987)

Carrol, N., 'A Select View of Earthlings: Ping Chong', *Drama Review*, vol. XXVII, no. 1 (1983) pp. 72–81.

Cheetham, M. A., with Hutcheon, L., *Remembering Postmodernism: Recent Trends in Canadian Art* (Oxford, 1991).

Connor, S., *Postmodernist Culture: An Introduction to Theories of the Contemporary* (Oxford, 1989).

Conrads, U., *Programmes and Manifestos on 20th Century Architecture* (London, 1970).

Demastes, W.W., 'Spalding Gray's *Swimming to Cambodia* and the Evolution of an Ironic Presence', *Theatre Journal*, vol. XXXXI, no. 1 (1989) pp. 75–94.

Derrida, J., *Of Grammatology* (London, 1974).

——, *Writing and Difference* (London, 1978).

Docherty, T., *After Theory: Post-modernism/Post-Marxism* (London, 1990).

Eco, U., *Reflections on 'The Name of the Rose'* (London, 1985).

——, *Travels in Hyperreality* (London, 1986).

——, *The Open Work*, 2nd edn (London, 1989).

Featherstone, M. (ed.), *Postmodernism* (London, 1988).

Ferguson, R., Olander, W., Ticker, M., and Fiss, K., *Discourses: Conversations in Postmodern Art and Culture* (New York, 1990).

Fokkema, D. W., and Bertens, J. W. (eds), *Approaching Postmodernism* (Amsterdam and Philadelphia, 1986).

Foster, H. (ed.), *Postmodern Culture* (London, 1983).

Gaggi, S., *Modern–Postmodern: A Study in Twentieth Century Arts and Ideas* (Philadelphia, Penn., 1989).

Goldberg, R., *Performance Art* (London, 1988).

Harvey, D., *The Condition of Postmodernity* (London, 1989).

Hassan, I., *The Dismemberment of Orpheus: Toward a Postmodern Literature* (Madison, Wisc., 1982).

——, *The Postmodern Turn: Essays in Postmodern Theory and Culture* (Columbus, Ohio, 1987).

Hutcheon, L., *A Poetics of Postmodernism: History, Theory, Fiction* (London, 1988).

——, *The Politics of Postmodernism* (London, 1989).

Huyssen, A., *After the Great Divide: Modernism, Mass Culture, Postmodernism* (Indianapolis, 1986).

Jameson, F., *Postmodernism, or, The Cultural Logic of Late Capitalism* (Durham, 1991).

Jencks, C., *What is Post-modernism?*, 2nd edn (London, 1987).

——, *Post-modernism: The New Classicism in Art and Architecture* (London, 1988).

——, *The Language of Postmodern Architecture* (London, 1977).

Kalb, J., 'Ping Chong: From *Lazarus* to *Anna into Nightlight*', *Theater*, vol. XIV, no. 2 (1983) pp. 68–75.

Kaplan, E. A., *Rocking Around the Clock: Music Television, Postmodernism and Consumer Culture* (London and New York, 1987).

—— (ed.), *Postmodernism and Its Discontents: Theories, Practices* (London, 1988).

Kaye, N., 'Richard Schechner: Theory and Practice of the Indeterminate Theatre', *New Theatre Quarterly*, vol. V, no. 20 (1989) pp. 348–60.

Klinkowitz, J., *Rosenberg, Barthes, Hassan: Postmodern Habit of Thought* (Athens, Ga, 1988).

Klotz, H., *The History of Postmodern Architecture* (London, 1988).

Krauss, R. E., *The Originality of the Avant-garde and Other Modernist Myths* (London, 1985).

Kroker, A., and Cook, D., *The Postmodern Scene: Excremental Culture and Hyper-aesthetics*, 2nd edn (London, 1988).

Lash, S., *Sociology of Postmodernism* (London, 1990).

Lawson, H., *Reflexivity: The Post-modern Predicament* (London, 1985).
Le Corbusier, *Towards a New Architecture* (London, 1927).
Lyotard, J.-F., *Discours, Figure* (Paris, 1971).
——, *The Differend: Phrases in Dispute* (Manchester, 1990).
——, *The Postmodern Condition: A Report on Knowledge* (Manchester, 1984).
——, and Thebaud, J.-L., *Just Gaming* (Manchester, 1985).
Madan, S., *An Introductory Guide to Post-structuralism and Post-modernism* (Athens, Ga, 1988).
Milner, A., Thompson, P., and Worth, C., *Postmodern Conditions* (Oxford, 1990).
Newman, C., *The Post-modern Aura* (Evanston, Ill., 1985).
Nicholson, L. J., *Feminism/Postmodernism* (London, 1990).
Norris, C., *What's Wrong with Postmodernism?: Critical Theory and the Ends of Philosophy* (London, 1990).
Papaport, H., ' "Can You Say Hello?": Laurie Anderson's *United States*', *Theatre Journal*, vol. XXXVIII, no. 3 (1986) pp. 339–54.
Paz, O., *Children of the Mire: Modern Poetry from Romanticism to the Avant-garde* (Cambridge, Mass., 1974).
Perloff, M. (ed.), *Postmodern Genres* (Norman, Okla, 1988).
Portoghesi, P., *Postmodern: The Architecture of Postindustrial Society* (New York, 1982).
Readings, B., *Introducing Lyotard: Art and Politics* (London, 1991).
Sayre, H., *The Object of Performance* (Chicago, 1989).
Schechner, R., *The End of Humanism* (New York, 1982).
Schleifer, R., *Rhetoric and Death: The Language of Modernism and Postmodern Discourse Theory* (Chicago, 1990)
Shapiro, G., *After the Future: Postmodern Times and Places* (New York, 1990).
Silverman, H. J. (ed.), *Postmodernism – Philosophy and the Arts* (London, 1990).
Tagg, J. (ed.), *The Cultural Politics of Postmodernism* (New York, 1989).
Trachtenberg, S. (ed.), *The Postmodern Moment: A Handbook of Contemporary Innovation in the Arts* (Westport, Conn., 1985).
Turner, B. S. (ed.), *Theories of Modernity and Postmodernity* (London, 1990).
Ulmer, G. L., *Applied Grammatology: Post(e)-Pedagogy from Jacques Derrida to Joseph Beuys* (Baltimore, md, 1981).
Vattimo, G., *The End of Modernity* (London, 1988).
Venturi, R., *Complexity and Contradiction in Architecture* (New York, 1966).
——, and Scott-Brown, D., *Learning from Las Vegas*, rev. edn (London, 1971).
Wakefield, N., *Postmodernism: The Twilight of the Real* (London, 1990).
Wright, E., *Postmodern Brecht: A Re-presentation* (London, 1988).

Theatricality and the modernist work

Battcock, G., *Minimal Art* (New York, 1968).
——, with Berger, R., and Glusberg, J., *The Art of Performance* (New York, 1979).
——, and Nickas, R. (eds), *The Art of Performance: A Critical Anthology* (New York, 1984).

Brecht, G., *Chance Imagery: A Great Bear Pamphlet* (New York, 1966).
———, and Fillou, R., *Games at the Cedilla, or The Cedilla Takes Off* (New York, 1967).
Bronson, A. A., and Gale, P., *Performance by Artists* (Toronto, 1979).
Buettner, S., *American Art Theory, 1945–1970* (Ann Arbor, Mich., 1981).
Cage, J., *Silence: Lectures and Writings* (Middletown, Conn., 1961).
Calder, J. (ed.), *New Writers Four* (London, 1967).
Crichton, M., *Jasper Johns* (London, 1977).
Fluxus, *1962 Wiesbaden Fluxus 1982* (Berlin, 1982).
Goldberg, R., *Performance Art* (London, 1979).
Greenberg, C., *Art and Culture* (Boston, Mass., 1965).
———, 'After Abstract Expressionism', *Art International*, vol. VI, no. 8 (1962) pp. 26–30.
———, 'Modernist Painting', *Art and Literature*, vol. 4 (1965) pp. 193–201.
Hansen, A., *A Primer of Happenings and Time/Space Art* (New York, 1965).
Hendricks, J. (ed.), *Fluxus Etc., The Gilbert and Lila Silverman Collection* (Bloomfield Hills, Mich., 1983).
Henri, A., *Environments and Happenings* (London, 1974).
Inga-Pin, L., *Performance, Happenings, Actions, Events, Activities, Installations* (Padua, 1978).
Johnson, E. H., *American Artists on Art* (New York, 1982).
Kaprow, A., *Assemblages, Environments and Happenings* (New York, 1966).
———, *Some Recent Happenings: A Great Bear Pamphlet* (New York, 1966).
———, 'The Happenings Are Dead: Long Live the Happenings', *Artforum*, vol. IV, no. 7 (1966) pp. 36–9.
———, *Untitled Essays and Other Works: A Great Bear Pamphlet* (New York, 1967).
———, 'Self-Service: a Happening', *Drama Review*, vol. XII, no. 3 (1968) pp. 160–4.
———, 'Education of the Un-artist, Part One', *Art News*, vol. LXIX, no. 10 (1971) pp. 28–31.
———, 'Education of the Un-artist, Part Two', *Art News*, vol. LXXI, no. 3 (1972) pp. 34–9, 62.
———, 'Education of the Un-artist, Part Three', *Art in America*, vol. LXII, no. 1 (1974) pp. 85-91.
———, 'Non-theatrical Performance', *Artforum*, vol. XIV, no. 9 (1976) pp. 45–51.
———, and R. Schechner, 'Extensions in Time and Space', *Drama Review*, vol. XII, no. 2 (1968) pp. 153–9.
Kostalanetz, R., *The Theatre of Mixed Means* (New York, 1968).
Loeffler, C. E., and Tung, D. (eds), *Performance Anthology: Source Book for a Decade of Californian Performance Art* (San Francisco, 1980).
Martin, H., *An Introduction to George Brecht's Book of the Tumbler on Fire* (Milan, 1978).
———, and Brecht, G., *A Conversation with George Brecht by Henry Martin* (Bologne, 1979).
Oldenburg, C., *Injun and Other Histories: A Great Bear Pamphlet* (New York, 1966).
———, *Store Days* (New York, 1967).
———, *Raw Notes* (Halifax, Nova Scotia, 1973).

Ruhe, H. (ed.), *Fluxus: the most radical and experimental art movement of the sixties* (Amsterdam, 1979).
Sohm, H. (ed.), *Happenings and Fluxus* (Cologne, 1970).

Kirby, Foreman, Wilson

Alenikoff, F., 'Scenario: a Talk with Robert Wilson', *Dance Scope*, vol. X, no. 1 (1975–61) pp. 11–21.
Andriessen, L., and Wilson, R., *Die Materie: Libretto* (Amsterdam, 1989).
Aronson, A., 'Wilson's *Dollar Value of Man*', *Drama Review*, vol. XIX, no. 3 (1975) pp. 106–10.
Baracks, B., 'Einstein on the Beach', *Artforum*, vol. XV, no. 7 (1977) pp. 30–6.
Bigsby, C. W. E., *A Critical Introduction to Twentieth Century American Drama*, vol. 3, *Beyond Broadway* (Cambridge, 1985).
Brecht, S., *The Theatre of Visions: Robert Wilson* (Frankfurt am Main, 1978).
Cage, J., Foreman, R., and Kostalanetz, R., 'Art in the Culture', *Performing Arts Journal*, vol. IV, nos 1 & 2 (1979) pp. 70–84.
Carroll, N., 'The Mystery Plays of Michael Kirby', *Drama Review*, vol. XXIII, no. 3 (1979) pp. 103–12.
Davy, K., 'Foreman's *Vertical Mobility* and *PAIN(T)*', *Drama Review*, vol. XVIII, no. 2 (1974) pp. 26–37.
——, 'Review: Foreman's *Pandering*', *Drama Review*, vol. XIX, no. 1 (1975) pp. 116–17.
——, 'Kate Manheim as Foreman's Rhoda', *Drama Review*, vol. XX, no. 3 (1976) pp. 37–50.
——, *Richard Foreman and the Ontological-Hysteric Theatre* (Ann Arbor, Mich., 1981).
—— (ed.), *Richard Foreman: Plays and Manifestos* (New York, 1976).
Deak, F., 'Robert Wilson', *Drama Review*, vol. XVIII, no. 2 (1974) pp. 67–80.
Donker, J., *The President of Paradise: A Traveller's Account of Robert Wilson's 'the CIVIL warS'* (Amsterdam, 1985).
Feingold, M., 'An Interview with Richard Foreman', *Theater*, vol. VII, no. 1 (1975) pp. 5–29.
Flakes, S., 'Robert Wilson's *Einstein on the Beach*', *Drama Review*, vol. XX, no. 4 (1976) pp. 69–82.
Foreman, R., '*Vertical Mobility*', *Drama Review*, vol. XVIII, no. 2 (1974) pp. 38–47.
——, 'How I Write My (Self: Plays)', *Drama Review*, vol. XXI, no. 4 (1977) pp. 5–24.
——, 'Hotel for Criminals', *Theater*, vol. VII, no. 1 (1975) pp. 30–55.
——, 'The American Imagination', *Performing Arts Journal*, vol. IV, nos 1 & 2 (1979) pp. 177–99.
——, *Reverberation Machines: The Later Plays and Essays* (New York, 1985).
——, 'Film is Ego: Radio is God', *Drama Review*, vol. XXXI, no. 4 (1987) pp. 149–76.
Glass, P., 'Notes: *Einstein on the Beach*', *Performing Arts Journal*, vol. II, no. 3 (1978) pp. 63–70.

Kaye, N., 'Bouncing Back the Impulse: an Interview with Richard Foreman', *Performance*, vol. 61 (1990) pp. 31–42.

Kirby, M., 'On Acting and Not Acting', *Drama Review*, vol. XVI, no. 1 (1972) pp. 3–15.

——,'Richard Foreman's Ontological-Hysteric Theatre', *Drama Review*, vol. XVII, no. 2 (1973) pp. 5–32.

——, 'Manifesto of Structuralism', *Drama Review*, vol. XIX, no. 4 (1975) pp. 82–3.

——, 'Structural Analysis/Structural Theory', *Drama Review*, vol. XX, no. 4 (1976) pp. 51–68.

——, *Photoanalysis: A Structuralist Play* (Seoul, 1978).

——, *First Signs of Decadence* (Schulenburg. 1986).

——, *A Formalist Theatre* (Philadelphia, 1987).

Langton, B., 'Journey to Ka Mountain', *Drama Review*, vol. XVII, no. 2 (1973) pp. 48–57.

Marranca, B., *Theatrewritings* (New York, 1984).

—— (ed.), *The Theatre of Images* (New York, 1977).

Nodal, A., and De Bretteville, S. L. (eds), *Robert Wilson's 'CIVIL warS': Drawings, Models and Documentation* (Los Angeles, 1984).

Monk, E., '*Film is Ego: Radio is God*, Richard Foreman and the Arts of Control', *Drama Review*, vol. XXXI, no. 4 (1987) pp. 143–8.

Nahston, E., 'With Foreman on Broadway', *Drama Review*, vol. XX, no. 3 (1976) pp. 83–100.

Quadri, F., 'Robert Wilson: It's About Time', *Artforum*, vol. XXIII, no. 2 (1984) pp. 76–82.

Rouse, J., 'Robert Wilson, Texts and History: *CIVIL warS*, German Part', *Theater*, vol. XVI, no. 1 (1984) pp. 68–74.

Savran, D., *In Their Own Words: Contemporary American Playwrights* (New York, 1988)

Scarpetta, G., 'Richard Foreman's Scenography: Examples of his Work in France', *Drama Review*, vol. XXVIII, no. 2 (1984) pp. 23–31.

Schechner, R., 'Richard Foreman on Richard Foreman', *Drama Review*, vol. XXXI, no. 4 (1987) pp. 125–35.

Shank, T., *American Alternative Theatre* (London, 1982).

Shyer, L., *Robert Wilson and His Collaborators* (New York, 1989).

Simmer, B., 'Robert Wilson and Therapy', *Drama Review*, vol. XX, no. 1 (1976) pp. 99–110.

——, 'Sue Sheehy', *Drama Review*, vol. XX, no. 3 (1976) pp. 67–74.

Trilling, O., 'Robert Wilson's *Ka Mountain*', *Drama Review*, vol. XVII, no. 2 (1973) pp. 33–47.

Wilson, R., 'I Thought I Was Hallucinating ...', *Drama Review*, vol. XXI, no. 4 (1977) pp. 75–8.

——, '*I Was Sitting on my Patio This Guy Appeared I Thought I Was Hallucinating*', *Performing Arts Journal*, vol. IV, nos 1 & 2 (1979) pp. 200–18.

——, *Robert Wilson: From a Theatre of Images* (Cincinatti, Ohio, 1980).

——, *The Golden Windows: A Play in Three Parts* (Munich, 1982).

——, and Knowles, C., '*The Dollar Value of Man*', *Theater*, vol. IX, no. 2 (1978) pp. 91–109.

Dance

Alter, J. B., 'A Critical Analysis of Susanne K. Langer's Dance Theory', *Dance Research Annual*, vol. XVI (1987) pp. 110–19.

Banes, S., *Democracy's Body: Judson Dance Theater, 1962–1964* (Ann Arbor, Mich., 1983).

——, *Terpsichore in Sneakers: Post-modern Dance*, 2nd edn (Middletown, Conn., 1987).

——, 'Vital Signs: Steve Paxton's *Flat* in Perspective', *Dance Research Annual*, vol. XVI (1987) pp. 120–34.

Beardsley, M. C., 'What is Going on in Dance?', *Dance Research Journal*, vol. XV, no. 1 (1982) pp. 31–6.

Brown, T., 'Three Pieces', *Drama Review*, vol. XIX, no. 1 (1975) pp. 26–33.

——, 'All of the Person's Person Arriving', *Drama Review*, vol. XXX, no. 1 (1986) pp. 149–70.

Brown, T., Brunel, L., Mangolte, B., and Delahaye, G., *l'atelier des chorégraphes Trisha Brown* (Paris, 1987).

Carrol, N., and Banes, S., 'Working and Dancing: a Response to Monroe C. Beardley's *What is Going on in Dance?*', *Dance Research Journal*, vol. XV, no. 1 (1982) pp. 37–'41.

Childs, L., 'Notes' 64–'74', *Drama Review*, vol. XIX, no. 1 (1975) pp. 33–6.

——, 'Lucinda Childs: a Portfolio', *Artforum*, vol. 11 (1973) pp. 50–7.

Chin, D., 'Talking with Lucinda Childs', *Dance Scope*, vol. XIII, nos 2 & 3 (1979) pp. 70–81.

Croce, A., *Afterimages* (New York, 1977).

Cunningham, M., *Changes: Notes on Choreography* (New York, 1968).

——, *The Dancer and the Dance* (London, 1985).

Fancher G., and Myers, G., *Philosophical Essays on Dance* (New York, 1981).

Forti, S., *Handbook in Motion* (Nova Scotia and New York, 1974).

Foster, S., 'The Signifying Body: Reaction and Resistance in Postmodern Dance', *Theatre Journal*, vol. XXXVII, no. 1 (1985) pp. 44–64.

——, *Reading Dancing: Bodies and Subjects in Contemporary American Dance* (Berkeley, Cal., 1986).

Goldberg, R., 'Space as Praxis', *Studio International*, vol. 977 (1975) pp. 130–5.

——, 'Performance: the Art of Notation', *Studio International*, vol. 982 (1976) pp. 54–8.

Gordon, D., 'It's About Time', *Drama Review*, vol. XIX, no. 1 (1975) pp. 43–52.

Goldwater, L., *Primitivism in Modern Art* (London, 1986).

Graham, M., *The Notebooks of Martha Graham* (New York, 1973).

Grand Union, 'The Grand Union', *Dance Scope*, vol. VII, no. 2 (1973) pp. 28–32.

Hay, D., 'Dance Talks', *Dance Scope*, vol. XII, no. 1 (1977–8) pp. 18–22.

Hecht, R., 'Reflections on the Career of Yvonne Rainer and the Value of Minimal Dance', *Dance Scope*, vol. VIII, no. 1 (1973–4) pp. 12–25.

Horst, L., *Pre-classic Dance Forms* (New York, 1968).

——, and Russell, C., *Modern Dance Forms* (San Francisco, 1961).

Humphrey, D., *The Art of Making Dance* (New York and Toronto, 1959).

Johnston, J., *Marmalade Me* (New York, 1971).

Sheets-Johnstone, M., 'On the Nature of Theories of Dance', *CORD Dance Research Annual*, vol. X (1979) pp. 3–29.

Kaprilian, M. H., 'What Makes Art Art?', *Dance Research Journal*, vol. XIX, no. 1 (1974–5) pp. 10–12.

Kirby, M., *The Art of Time* (New York, 1969).

——, 'The New Dance: an Introduction', *Drama Review*, vol. XVI, no. 3 (1972) pp. 115–16.

Langer, S. K., *Feeling and Form: A Theory of Art* (London, 1953).

Livet, A., *Contemporary Dance* (New York, 1978).

Lorber, R., 'The Problem with the Grand Union', *Dance Scope*, vol. VIII, no. 2 (1973) pp. 33–4.

Manning, S., 'Modernist Dogma and "Post-modern" Rhetoric: a Response to Sally Banes' *Terpsichore in Sneakers*', *Drama Review*, vol. XXXIV, no. 4 (1988) pp. 32–9.

Martin, J., *The Modern Dance* (New York, 1933).

——, *Introduction to the Dance* (New York, 1939).

Mazo, J. H., *Prime Movers* (London, 1977).

McDonagh, D., *The Rise and Fall and Rise of Modern Dance* (New York, 1970).

Michelson, A., 'Yvonne Rainer, Part 1: The Dancer and the Dance', *Artforum*, vol. XII, no. 5 (1974) pp. 57–63.

Morris, R., 'Notes on Dance', *Tulane Drama Review*, vol. X, no. 2 (1965) pp. 179–86.

Nadel, M. H. and Miller, C. N., *The Dance Experience: Readings in Dance Appreciation* (New York, 1978).

Paxton, S., 'The Grand Union', *Drama Review*, vol. XVI, no. 3 (1972) pp. 128–34.

Percival, L., *Experimental Dance* (London, 1971).

Rainer, Y., 'Yvonne Rainer Interviews Anne Halprin', *Drama Review*, vol. X, no. 2 (1965) pp. 142–67.

——, *Work, 1961–73* (Nova Scotia and New York, 1974).

——, with Hulton, P., and Fulkerson, M., *Dartington Theatre Papers*, series 2, Number 7: *Yvonne Rainer* (Dartington Hall, Devon, 1978).

Sachs, C., *World History of the Dance* (New York, 1937).

Segal, M., 'Yvonne Rainer: Holding a Mirror to Experience', *Studio International*, vol. 982 (1976) pp. 41–3.

Schmit, S., 'Off Off Broadway: Three Chances at Judson', *Village Voice*, 8 March 1962.

Siegel, M. B., 'Modern Dance Before Bennington: Sorting It All Out', *Dance Research Journal*, vol. XIX, no. 1 (1987) pp. 3–9.

Smith, K., 'David Gordon's *The Matter*', *Drama Review*, vol. XIX, no. 1 (1972) pp. 117–27.

Sommer, S. R., 'Equipment Dances: Trisha Brown', *Drama Review*, vol. XIX, no. 1 (1972) pp. 135–41.

——, 'Trisha Brown: Making Dances', *Dance Scope*, vol. XI, no. 2 (1977) pp. 7–18.

Stefano, E., 'Moving Structures', *Art and Artists*, vol. VIII, no. 10 (1974) pp. 16–25.

Steinman, L., *The Knowing Body: Elements of Contemporary Performance* (Boston, Mass., 1986).

Sulzman, M., 'Choice/Form in Trisha Brown's *Locus*: a View from Inside the Cube', *Dance Chronicle*, vol. II, no. 2 (1978) pp. 117–30.

Telling stories

Aronson, A., 'Sakonnet Point', *Drama Review*, vol. XIX, no. 4 (1975) pp. 27–35.
——, 'The Wooster Group's *L. S. D. (... Just the High Points ...)*, *Drama Review*, vol. XXIX, no. 2 (1985) pp. 65–77.
Auslander, P., 'Toward a Concept of the Political in Postmodern Theatre', *Theatre Journal*, vol. XXXIX, no. 1 (1987) pp. 20–34.
——, 'Task and Vision: Willem Dafoe in *L. S. D.*', *Drama Review*, vol. XXIX, no. 2 (1985) pp. 94–8.
Bierman, J., 'Three Places in Rhode Island', *Drama Review*, vol. XXXIII, no. 1 (1989) pp. 13–30.
Borden, L., 'Trisha Brown and Yvonne Rainer', *Artforum*, vol. XI, no. 10 (1973) pp. 79–82.
Bos, S., 'Interview with Joan Jonas', *De Appel Bulletin*, vol. 1 (1985).
Burbank, R. J., *Thornton Wilder*, 2nd edn (New York, 1978).
Carr, C., 'Karen Finley', *Artforum*, vol. XXVII, no. 3 (1988) p. 148.
Champagne, L., 'Always Starting Anew: Elizabeth LeCompte', *Drama Review*, vol. XXV, no. 3 (1981) pp. 19–28.
——, *Out From Under: Texts by Women Performance Artists* (New York, 1990)
Christie, I., 'Lives of Performers', *Monthly Film Bulletin*, vol. XXXX, no. 520 (1977) pp. 101.
Coco, W., 'Review: *Route 1 & 9*', *Theatre Journal*, vol. XXXIV, no. 2 (1982) pp. 249–52.
——, and Gunawarda, A. J., 'Responses to India: an Interview with Yvonne Rainer', *Drama Review*, vol. XV, no. 3 (1971) pp. 139–42.
Coe, R., 'Four Performance Artists', *Theater*, vol. XII, no. 2 (1982) pp. 76–85.
Dimmick, K., 'Who's Afraid of LSD?', *Theater*, vol. XVI, no. 2 (1985) pp. 92–6.
Dolan J., *The Feminist Spectator as Critic* (Ann Arbor, Mich., 1988).
Erickson, J., 'Appropriation and Transgression in Contemporary American Performance: the Wooster Group, Holly Hughes and Karen Finley', *Theatre Journal*, vol. XLII, no. 2 (1990) pp. 225–36.
Finley, K., *Shock Treatment* (San Francisco, 1990).
——, 'The Constant State of Desire', *Drama Review*, vol. XXXII, no. 1 (1988) pp. 139–51.
Forte, J., 'Women's Performance Art: Feminism and Postmodernism', *Theatre Journal*, vol. XXXX, no. 2 (1988) pp. 217–36.
Fuchs, E., 'Performance Notes: *North Atlantic* and *L. S. D.*', *Performing Arts Journal*, vol. VIII, no. 2 (1984) pp. 51–5
——, 'Staging the Obscene Body', *Drama Review*, vol. XXXIII, no. 1 (1989) pp. 33–58.
Gray, S., 'About *Three Places in Rhode Island*', *Drama Review*, vol. XXXIII, no. 1 (1989) pp. 31–42.
——, and LeCompte, E., 'The Making of a Trilogy', *Performing Arts Journal*, vol. III, no. 2 (1978) pp. 81–91.
——, 'Rumstick Road', *Performing Arts Journal*, vol. III, no. 2 (1978) pp. 92–115.
Hart, L., 'Motherhood According to Finley: *The Theory of Total Blame*', *Drama Review*, vol. XXXVI, no. 1 (1992) pp. 124–34.

Howell, J., 'The Constant Stage of Desire', *Artforum*, vol. XXV, no. 7 (1987) pp. 130–11.

Hulton, P., 'Fiction, Character and Narrative: Yvonne Rainer' (interview), *Dartington Theatre Papers*, 2nd series, no. 7 (Dartington Hall, Devon, 1978).

Jonas, J., 'Seven Years', *Drama Review*, vol. XIX, no. 1 (1975) pp. 13–17.

——, *Joan Jonas' Stage Sets* (Philadelphia, 1976).

——, *Scripts and Descriptions, 1968–1982* (Berekeley, Cal., 1983).

——, and White, R., 'Interview with Joan Jonas', *View*, vol. II, no. 1 (1979) whole issue.

Jong, C. de, 'Organic Honey's Visual Telepathy', *Drama Review*, vol. XVI, no. 2 (1972) pp. 63–5.

Kaye, N., 'Mask, Role and Narrative: an Interview with Joan Jonas', *Performance*, vols 65–6 (1992) pp. 49–60.

King, B., *Contemporary American Theatre* (London, 1991).

Koch, S., 'Performance: a Conversation', *Artforum*, vol. XI, no. 4 (1972) pp. 53–8.

LeCompte, E., 'The Wooster Group Dances', *Drama Review*, vol. XXXIX, no. 2 (1985) pp. 78–93.

Michelson, A., 'Yvonne Rainer, Part 2: Lives of Performers', *Artforum*, vol. XII, no. 6 (1974) pp. 30–5.

Nadotti, M., 'Karen Finley's Poison Meatloaf', *Artforum*, vol. XXXVII, no. 7 (1989) pp. 113–16.

Rainer, Y., *The Films of Yvonne Rainer* (Indianapolis, 1989).

——, *Work, 1961–73* (Nova Scotia, 1974).

Riering, J., 'Joan Jonas: Delay Delay', *Drama Review*, vol. XVI, no. 3 (1972) pp. 142–51.

Robinson, M., 'Performance Strategies: Interviews with Ishmael Huston-Joanes, John Kelly, Karen Finley, Richard Elovich', *Performing Arts Journal*, vol. X, no. 3 (1987) pp. 31–56.

Savran, D., 'The Wooster Group, Arthur Miller and *The Crucible*', *Drama Review*, vol. XXIX, no. 2 (1985) pp. 99–109.

——, *The Wooster Group, 1975–1985: Breaking the Rules* (New York, 1988).

Schechner, R., 'Karen Finley: a Constant State of Becoming', *Drama Review*, vol. XXXII, no. 1 (1988) pp. 152–8.

Schuler, C., 'Spectator Response and Comprehension: the Problem of Karen Finley's *Constant State of Desire*', *Drama Review*, vol. XXXIV, no. 1 (1990) pp. 131–45.

Stofflet, M., 'Joan Jonas and Cultural Biography', *Artweek*, 7 June 1980, p. 5

——, 'Jonas' Futurism', *Artweek*, 6 July 1980 p. 5.

Welling, J., 'Joan Jonas Performance', *Artweek*, 12 April 1975, p. 4.

Wohl, D., 'The Wooster Group's *North Atlantic*', *Theatre Journal*, vol. XXXVI, no. 3 (1984) pp. 413–15.

Index

KING ALFRED'S COLLEGE
LIBRARY